Learn Apache Mesos

A beginner's guide to scalable cluster management and deployment

Manuj Aggarwal

BIRMINGHAM - MUMBAI

Learn Apache Mesos

Copyright © 2018 Packt Publishing

Commissioning Editor: Pravin Dhandre
Acquisition Editor: Divya Poojari
Content Development Editor: Karan Thakkar
Technical Editor: Dinesh Pawar
Copy Editor: Safis Editing
Project Coordinator: Nidhi Joshi
Proofreader: Safis Editing
Indexer: Pratik Shirodkar
Graphics: Jisha Chirayil
Production Coordinator: Nilesh Mohite

First published: October 2018

Production reference: 1311018

Published by Packt Publishing Ltd.
Livery Place
35 Livery Street
Birmingham
B3 2PB, UK.

ISBN 978-1-78913-738-5

www.packtpub.com

`mapt.io`

Mapt is an online digital library that gives you full access to over 5,000 books and videos, as well as industry leading tools to help you plan your personal development and advance your career. For more information, please visit our website.

Why subscribe?

- Spend less time learning and more time coding with practical eBooks and Videos from over 4,000 industry professionals

- Improve your learning with Skill Plans built especially for you

- Get a free eBook or video every month

- Mapt is fully searchable

- Copy and paste, print, and bookmark content

Packt.com

Did you know that Packt offers eBook versions of every book published, with PDF and ePub files available? You can upgrade to the eBook version at `www.packt.com` and as a print book customer, you are entitled to a discount on the eBook copy. Get in touch with us at `customercare@packtpub.com` for more details.

At `www.packt.com`, you can also read a collection of free technical articles, sign up for a range of free newsletters, and receive exclusive discounts and offers on Packt books and eBooks.

Contributors

About the author

Manuj Aggarwal is an entrepreneur, investor, and technology enthusiast. Over the last few years, he has been a business owner, technical architect, CTO, coder, start up consultant, and more.

Currently, he is the principal consultant, architect, and CTO of a software consulting company, TetraNoodle Technologies, based in Vancouver, Canada. He works with various start-ups on a number of cutting edge and interesting problems. Whether it is ideation and the refining of your start up idea, or building a dream team to execute the idea, he provides a diverse set of solutions that help these start-ups to succeed in their plans.

He has been active in the software industry since 1997, and has worked with early-stage businesses through to Fortune 100 mega-corporations. He is passionate about sharing all the knowledge that he has acquired over the years. He is particularly interested in helping technical and non-technical entrepreneurs, founders, and co-founders of tech start-ups.

Packt is searching for authors like you

If you're interested in becoming an author for Packt, please visit `authors.packtpub.com` and apply today. We have worked with thousands of developers and tech professionals, just like you, to help them share their insights with the global tech community. You can make a general application, apply for a specific hot topic that we are recruiting an author for, or submit your own idea.

Table of Contents

Preface

Apache Mesos is an open source cluster manager that provides efficient resource isolation and sharing across distributed applications. *Learn Apache Mesos* dives straight into how Mesos works. You will be introduced to distributed systems and their challenges, and then understand how you can use Mesos and its framework to solve data problems. You will also gain a full understanding of Mesos' internal mechanisms and get equipped to use Mesos and develop applications. Furthermore, this book lets you explore all the steps required to create highly available clusters and build your own Mesos frameworks. You will also cover application deployment and monitoring.

You will learn how Mesos works and then develop applications. You will learn to make full use of machines and simplify the maintenance of a data center with Mesos.

Who this book is for

This book is for DevOps, data engineers, and administrators who work with large data clusters. You'll also find this book useful if you have experience of working with virtualization, databases, and platforms such as Hadoop and Spark. Some experience in database administration and design will help you get the most out of this book.

What this book covers

Chapter 1, *Deploying Apache Mesos on AWS*, contains an overview of the Mesos architecture and how Mesos helps different teams to enhance their performance and deliver on it.

Chapter 2, *Setting up Mesos Single-Cluster Nodes*, explains how to set up AWS servers and how to deploy Mesos and its components.

Chapter 3, *Installation of Mesosphere*, explores the components that comprise a Mesos cluster.

Chapter 4, *Apache Mesos Administration*, explains how Mesos schedules resources, and how its allocation module offers those resources to various frameworks.

Chapter 5, *Deploying Services on Mesos Cluster*, shows how to start working on a Mesos cluster and how to deploy applications.

Chapter 6, *Persistent Volumes*, explains how to set up and use SSL to protect important endpoints. It also explains how to choose suitable authentication mechanisms.

Chapter 7, *Securing Mesos*, explains how to debug and troubleshoot the services and workloads on a Mesos cluster.

Chapter 8, *Managing Resources in Mesos*, explains how to manage CPU, memory, and disk resources in a Mesos environment.

To get the most out of this book

For this book, you will require a prior basic knowledge of SSH, AWS, and Mesos, and you will also require an AWS subscription.

Download the example code files

You can download the example code files for this book from your account at www.packt.com. If you purchased this book elsewhere, you can visit www.packt.com/support and register to have the files emailed directly to you.

You can download the code files by following these steps:

1. Log in or register at www.packt.com.
2. Select the **SUPPORT** tab.
3. Click on **Code Downloads & Errata**.
4. Enter the name of the book in the **Search** box and follow the onscreen instructions.

Once the file is downloaded, please make sure that you unzip or extract the folder using the latest version of:

- WinRAR/7-Zip for Windows
- Zipeg/iZip/UnRarX for Mac
- 7-Zip/PeaZip for Linux

The code bundle for the book is also hosted on GitHub at https://github.com/ PacktPublishing/Learn-Apache-Mesos. In case there's an update to the code, it will be updated on the existing GitHub repository.

We also have other code bundles from our rich catalog of books and videos available at https://github.com/PacktPublishing/. Check them out!

Download the color images

We also provide a PDF file that has color images of the screenshots/diagrams used in this book. You can download it here: http://www.packtpub.com/sites/default/files/downloads/9781789137385_ColorImages.pdf.

Conventions used

There are a number of text conventions used throughout this book.

CodeInText: Indicates code words in text, database table names, folder names, filenames, file extensions, pathnames, dummy URLs, user input, and Twitter handles. Here is an example: "So, we will give 10.0.0.0/16. Keep the IPv6 CIDR block as default."

Any command-line input or output is written as follows:

```
Ssh -I "mesos.pem" root@34.201.25.46
```

Bold: Indicates a new term, an important word, or words that you see on screen. For example, words in menus or dialog boxes appear in the text like this. Here is an example: "Set **Tenancy** as **Default**."

Warnings or important notes appear like this.

Tips and tricks appear like this.

Get in touch

Feedback from our readers is always welcome.

General feedback: If you have questions about any aspect of this book, mention the book title in the subject of your message and email us at customercare@packtpub.com.

Errata: Although we have taken every care to ensure the accuracy of our content, mistakes do happen. If you have found a mistake in this book, we would be grateful if you would report this to us. Please visit www.packt.com/submit-errata, selecting your book, clicking on the Errata Submission Form link, and entering the details.

Piracy: If you come across any illegal copies of our works in any form on the Internet, we would be grateful if you would provide us with the location address or website name. Please contact us at copyright@packt.com with a link to the material.

If you are interested in becoming an author: If there is a topic that you have expertise in and you are interested in either writing or contributing to a book, please visit authors.packtpub.com.

Reviews

Please leave a review. Once you have read and used this book, why not leave a review on the site that you purchased it from? Potential readers can then see and use your unbiased opinion to make purchase decisions, we at Packt can understand what you think about our products, and our authors can see your feedback on their book. Thank you!

For more information about Packt, please visit packt.com.

Deploying Apache Mesos on AWS

1

In the IT world today, some of the types of applications being developed cannot survive on a single computer. This is because these applications are accessed by a large number of users. Also, different types of applications means different platforms, such as Java and .NET.

Apache Mesos is a concentrated fault-tolerant cluster-management tool that is used for distributed computing environments that provides resource-isolation and management across a cluster of slave nodes. It efficiently manages the CPU memory and disk resources across the cluster, schedules the resources according to requirements, and deploys the apps. It is a highly available master through Apache ZooKeeper.

Apart from this, Apache Mesos also provides features such as application scheduling, scaling, faulttolerance, and cellfilling. It also supplies an application service discovery tool.

In this chapter, we will cover the following topics:

- Installation and configuration of a highly available cluster in Apache Mesos
- Setting the failure configuration in case the master nodes go down
- Setting up a Mesos slave server to handle the Docker-related tasks, which are scheduled by Marathon

Introduction to Apache Mesos

Imagine an e-commerce application server where, if you are selling a product, lots of users access your website. This creates a huge amount of data and requires more CPU memory and disk space. Day-by-day users increase, so the demand for resources increases. To cater to these needs, you use data centers and the cloud to provide these additional resources. Apache Mesos helps to manage and share these resources in an efficient manner, and also helps us with scalable deployments by forming a cluster.

A Mesos cluster is made up of four major components:

- ZooKeeper
- Mesos masters
- Mesos slaves
- Frameworks

Architecture of Mesos

Mesos has an architecture with the combination of master and slave daemons and frameworks. Here are a few definitions of components used in our architecture:

- **Master daemon**: Mesos master runs on a master node and organizes the slave daemons, so we will have three master nodes where we will install Mesos master, and it will manage the Mesos slave server, which runs on the other three servers.
- **Slave daemon**: Mesos slave runs on slave nodes and runs tasks that belong to the framework, so we will be having a Marathon framework, which will register with the Mesos master and will schedule the Docker containers, and those Docker containers will run on Mesos slave servers.
- **Framework**: The framework, which can also be called the Mesos application, consists of a scheduler, which registers with the master to achieve resource offers, and one or more executors, which pushes the tasks on slaves. An example of a Mesos framework is Marathon. The Marathon framework can be used in the scheduling of tasks. So, the Marathon framework gets registered with the Mesos master and it receives the resource offers. This framework also deploys the application on the Mesos cluster, which gets launched on slaves.

Following are other important components of the Mesos architecture:

- **Offer**: The master gets offers from the slave nodes and the master provides offers to the registered frameworks. So, all the resources are on slave node, such as CPU memory and disk, and then the Mesos master provides offers to the registered framework, which is Marathon.
- **Task**: A unit of work that is scheduled by a framework, Marathon, and tasks are like Docker. If we run any image of Docker, those Docker images will run on a slave node. Tasks can be anything, from a bash command, or script, or running a Docker container.
- **Apache ZooKeeper**: It's a software that is used to coordinate the master nodes. It elects the master leader, and if out of three nodes any node is down, it again elects the leader from the remaining two nodes. A minimum of three nodes is required to form a cluster.

Introduction to Amazon Web Service (AWS)

AWS is a secured cloud service platform that offers computing power. This is where we can run an EC2 instance for our master and slave, and then for the Marathon framework. It offers database storage as well.

We will use a MySQL database that offers more functionality to help the environment scale and grow.

AWS environment

For creating a VPC, EC2 instance, security groups, and load-balancers, perform the following steps:

1. Create a Virtual Private Cloud:

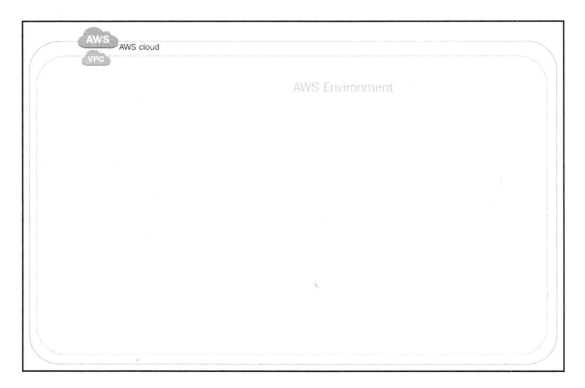

2. Create an EC2 instance: two for Marathon, three for Mesos master servers, and three for the Mesos slave servers:

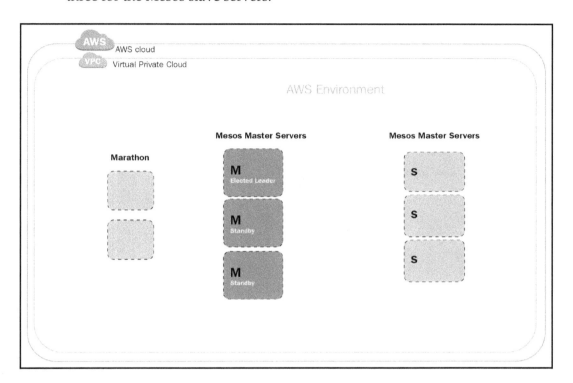

3. Install the Mesos master application, Marathon:

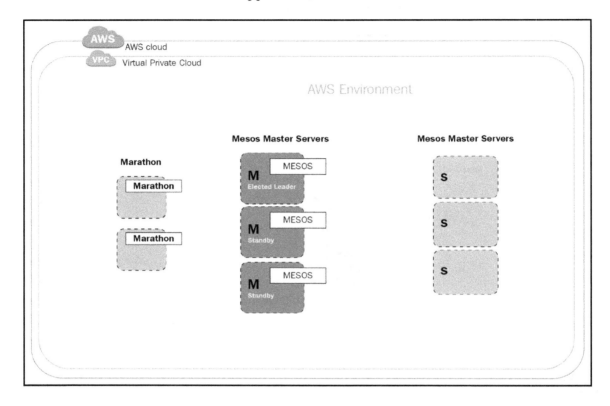

4. Install ZooKeeper:

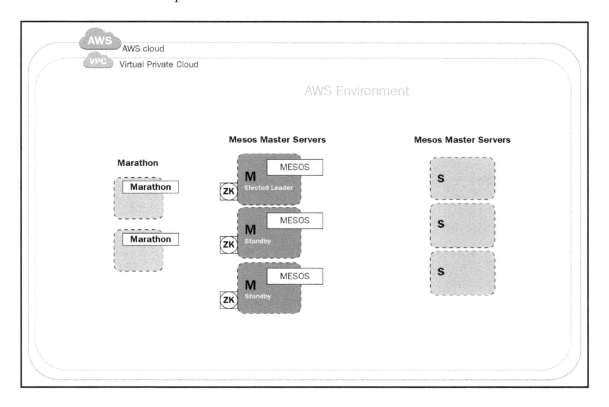

5. Insert Docker to run Docker images on all the slave servers. We will install the Mesos slave as well:

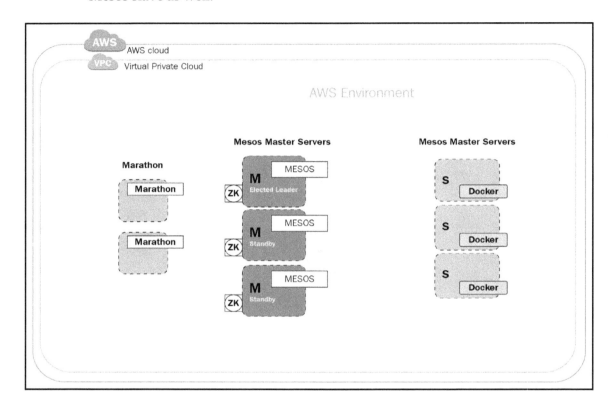

6. Use Marathon to deploy the application, and those tasks will launch on slave servers. We will use a WordPress Docker container:

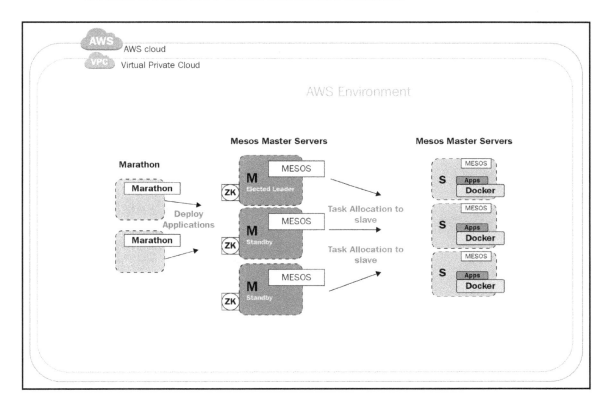

Also, we will see how to load-balance Marathon and Mesos master servers. This will help to manage the Mesos UI and Marathon UI. It is not necessary to go every time on each Marathon server as the load-balancer will take care of that. If one of the master servers is down, it will redirect to another one, so this is where your management will become easy:

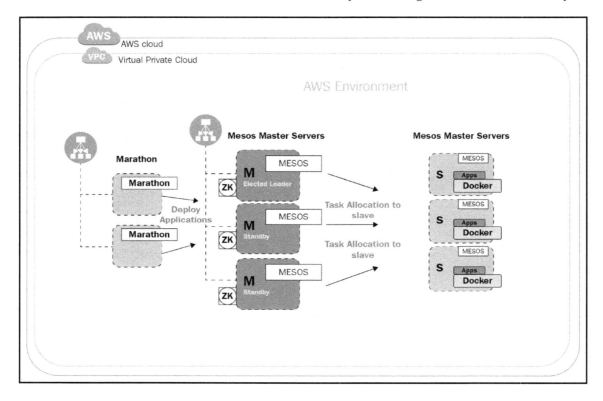

Use Marathon-lb HAProxy to load-balance your application request:

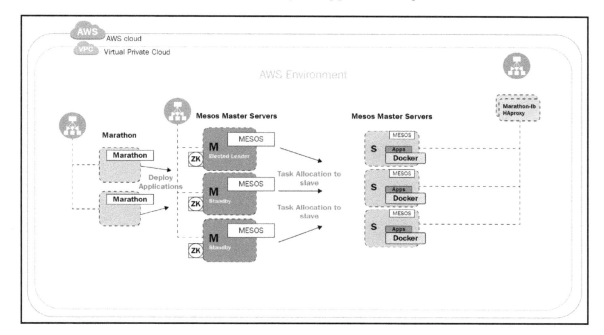

This was a quick overview of what we are going to cover in the upcoming chapters.

Summary

In this chapter, we explored the components of Apache Mesos. We also went through the overall architecture of Mesos. Then we covered the procedure of setting up an AWS environment.

In the next chapter, we will learn how to set up a Mesos single-cluster node. We will discuss some of the considerations in setting up a development environment. We will also use minimum server to deploy Mesos components for development purposes to build a development environment for Mesos using a Mesos single-cluster node setup.

2
Setting up Mesos Single-Cluster Nodes

In this chapter, we will discuss some of the considerations for setting up a development environment. The minimum server is used to deploy Mesos components for development purposes.

Our intention here is to build a development environment for Mesos by using a Mesos single-cluster-node setup, along with installing and configuring Mesos components on a single node, in the following order:

- Setting up servers on AWS
- Adding the Mesosphere repository in CentOS
- Installing a single instance of ZooKeeper
- Installing Mesos master services
- Installing Mesos slave services
- Installing the Docker engine
- Installing Marathon
- Deploying a sample application
- Enabling inbound traffic using security groups to access Mesos and the Marathon console

Setup of servers on AWS

To deploy Apache Mesos and the pertinent components, we need servers where we can install these components. So, in this module, we will work on creating EC2 instances on AWS.

To deploy Mesos on AWS, we should have a **Virtual Private Cloud** (**VPC**), a subnet, in order to launch our instances inside different subnets as per our requirements, a route table where our instances can communicate with each other, and an internet gateway for public access, and then we will create the EC2 instances. After the creation of EC2 instances, we will deploy our Mesos software and their components.

Before we start with EC2 instances, let's understand the architecture of our system. The following diagram shows the architecture in which we are working on AWS and creating a VPC. Now we will create the EC2 instance, which will have two Marathon servers and three Mesos master servers along with Mesos slave servers. This will be around eight servers where Mesos will be installed.

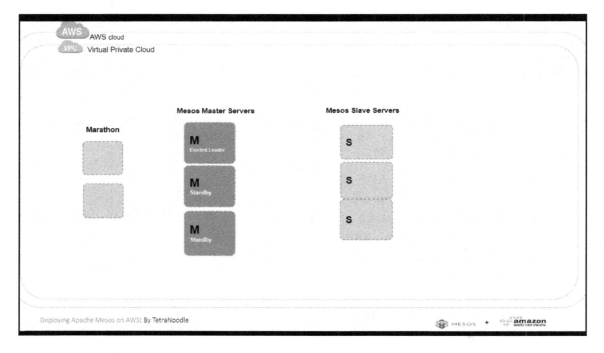

Let's get started by setting up the AWS servers.

Creating a VPC on AWS

In order to set up servers on AWS, perform the following steps:

1. Log in to your AWS console and click on Your VPCs.

2. In order to create a new one, click on **Create VPC** and name it `Mesos` (since we are working on installing Mesos). Provide a IP in CIDR block text. The CIDR block is the range of the IP address that we want to create the subnet of, and then on each subnet we will have own IP address that our instances can use when launched in each subnet. So, we will put `10.0.0.0/16`. Keep the IPv6 CIDR block as the default and set **Tenancy** as **Default**. Here, default means resources can run on shared hardware. As you are running on shared hardware, Amazon provides complete security for your VPC. Click on **Yes, Create**:

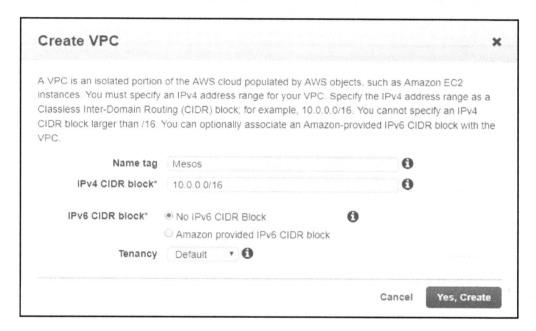

The following screenshot shows the created VPC:

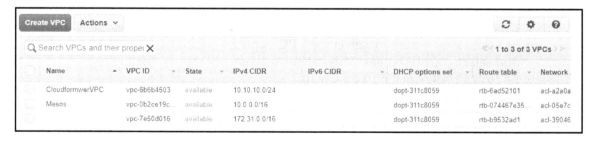

Our next step will be to create subnets.

Creating subnets

Subnets contain the instance resource and will have their own IP address ranges. So, when creating subnets, you should know how you will leverage the AWS availability zone. This will help us to create a reliable and available infrastructure for our application. In order to create the subnets, perform the following steps:

1. Click on the **Subnets** tab present at the sidebar. Set the **Name tag** as `10.0.1.0-mesos`; this will help us to identify our subnet easily. Then we will select our VPC, which was created earlier, as shown:

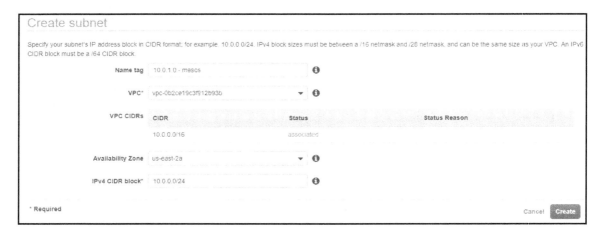

2. Create the availability zone. On selecting the drop-down, you can see there are six different availability zones. Here, we can create highly available servers on AWS, that is, **us-east-1a**.
3. Select the CIDR block that will be our IP range: `10.0.1.0/24`. By giving this IP address, our subnet will have IP address from `10.0.0.1`, `1.1`, `1.2`, `1.3`, and so on. Click **Yes, Create** to create the subnet.
4. Create one more subnet by clicking the **Create Subnet** tab and set the **Name tag** as `10.0.2.0 - mesos`, select the VPC, set the availability zone as **us-east-1b**, and select your IP ranges. This subnet will have IP ranges starting from `10.0.2.0/24`. Click on **Yes, Create.**

5. We have created two subnets:

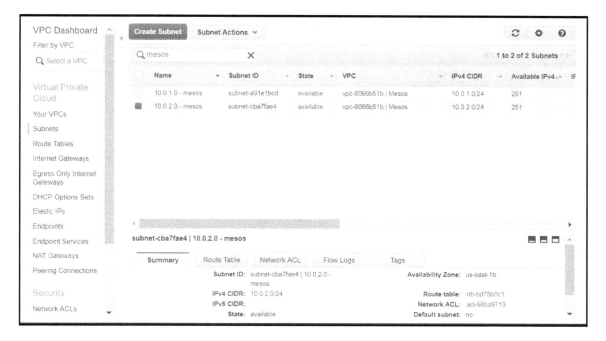

Now let's go ahead and check out route tables.

Creating a route table

Once we select **Route Tables** option on the left pane, we can see we already have a default route created for our VPC. When we created `vpc-6066b51b`, this route table was created:

The route table will help us to flow our traffic between the subnets. As we have created two subnets, this route table will help us to communicate between two subsets.

Click on the **Subnets** option, and on the **Route Table** tab you will find that our subnet is correctly associated with our route table, which is `rtb-bd75b0c1`:

You can cross-verify the route table by visiting the route table and checking the name of our VPC.

You probably will have noticed that the **Target** is **local**, which means any route inside this IP range will get routed and traffic will be served.

We will now work on creating our servers.

Creating EC2 instances

Now we will create the EC2 instances for our Mesos application. You will see running instance details on the EC2 dashboard:

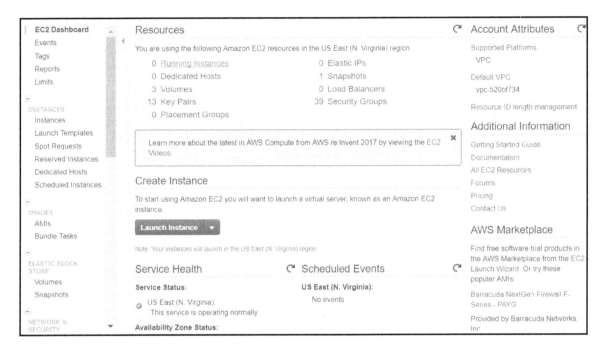

Since at present we do not have any instances running, you will find it blank. Let's create instances for our Mesos application to be deployed on those servers.

Click on **INSTANCES** (on the sidebar) and click **Launch Instances**. This will direct you to the page for you to select the type of instances you want. For this example, we are using CentOS. To use CentOS, we need to go the marketplace and search CentOS. Select the CentOS 7 module and then click on **Continue**:

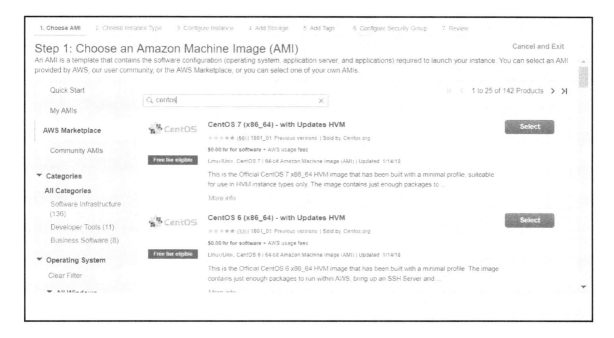

In the following screen, we will use general-purpose instance, which is free-tier eligible. On the following screen, we need to provide a few details to create the instance, such as network, number of instances, and select the VPC and one of the two subnets. Set the **Auto-assign Public IP** to **Enable**. We will keep the rest of the fields we will be keeping as default:

We have to create eight instances, that is, two for Marathon, three for Mesos master, and three for slave. However, for the subnet that we selected, will be providing one for Marathon, two for Mesos master, and one for slave, which is a total of five instances. Then we need to select the VPC that was created earlier and any of the subnets. Here we have selected the 10.0.1.0 subnet. Click on **Next: Add Storage**.

The following screen displays the **Volume Type**, **Device**, and **Snapshot** details that will be created by default. We will be using only 8 GB of space. Now we will change the **Volume Type** to **General Purpose** and click on **Next**. This will lead you to the **Add tags** page, which we will not be providing at present, so click **Next** to go to **Security Group**. Here we will allow only port 22, and change the **Security Group** name to **Mesos**. We are allowing port range as 22 only to access our server. The source can be any destination, but you can restrict to your public IP from where you want access to the server and then click the **Review** and **Launch** button. This screen will show you a summary of your selections. You can cross-verify and review the servers, number of instance files to provide storage details, and the tags, if you have any. Click on **Launch**:

Here you need to create a new key pair with **mesos** as the key pair name. Click on **Download Key Pair**, as shown in the screenshot. It will be required to log into the servers later, and then click on **Launch Instances**. It will take a few minutes for the instances to be created:

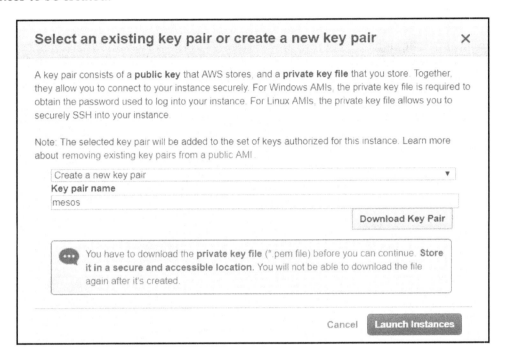

Now let's check our EC2 instances. You will find all our five instances have been created and in the Initializing phase, so let's wait till it gets launched or started. The following screenshot shows that our checks are complete and our instances are in the running phase:

Now we will try to connect to our server. You will see it has all the details when you select any of the instances. You can find the IP address, Public IP, and the Private IP under the **Description** tab. Note that the IP in our case is 34.239.228.166. Copy it, and we will use PuTTY to log in to the server. Enter the IP that you just copied and click on **Open**:

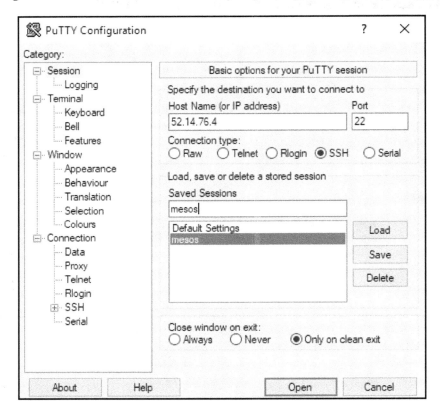

You will notice that we are not able to log in to the server. This is because our VPC is not exposed to the public. To do that, we should have the internet gateway attached to our VPC so our servers can connect to the server and are exposed on a public network, and we can access it. Let's create an internet gateway and attach it to our VPC. In the VPC Dashboard, select **Internet Gateways**, then **Create Internet Gateway**, and name it mesos:

On creating the gateways, you can see that it is in detached mode. We need to attach this internet gateway to our VPC. To attach the VPC to our gateway, right-click on the created gateway, click our VPC, and click on the **Yes, Attach** button. To provide internet access to our instances, we need to add another route to the table. Go to **Route Tables**, and under **Routes**, click on **Add another route**. In the **Target** we select our internet gateway, which we created, and our destination can be anything; we are keeping it as 0.0.0.0/0. We have now added another route. Now click on **Subnets**. We need to make sure this route is attached to our subnet so it can have access to the internet. Remember the route table, which is bd75b0c1. Under the subnet, you can see our route is already been added because we have already attached this route table to our subnet earlier. This creates a route to connect to our internet gateway in order to access the internet:

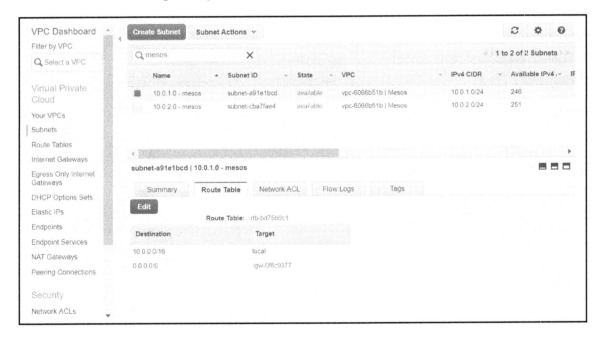

Let's again check whether we can access the instances using SSH. Go to **EC2 Instances**, click on any of the instances, and grab one of the IP addresses. Then, open PuTTY, load your configuration that was downloaded earlier, put in the IP address of the instances, and click on **Open**. You will be asked for login credentials. That means we have successfully connected our instance to the internet and now we can log in to the instances. Enter user as `centos`, and press *Enter*. So, in the following way you can access your instances on the internet using an internet gateway:

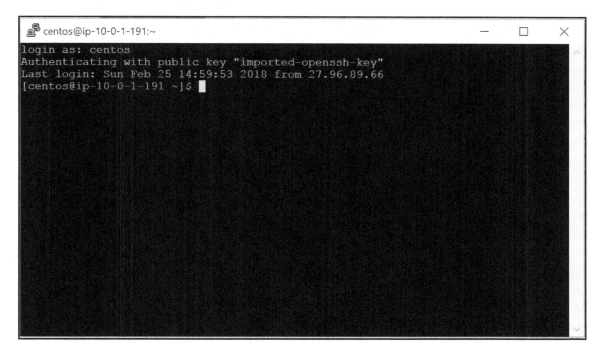

Here we have used PuTTY to connect, but if you are using a Linux Terminal, you can easily use SSH, right-click on the instance, and click on **Connect**. It will show you how you can use your PEM to connect to your server. Here is an example command to connect to the SSH:

```
Ssh -I "mesos.pem" root@34.201.25.46
```

However, in our case, first we need to convert your PEM to your PPK, which is the private key. You will find a different converter online, one of which will be PuTTYgen. In PuTTYgen, you first need to load the PEM file and save it as a PPK. Once you have converted the file, open PuTTY, expand the SSH, go in the **Auth** menu, and add the path to the PPK file that was converted. You can now connect to the instances using PuTTY by selecting the method and clicking on **Open**:

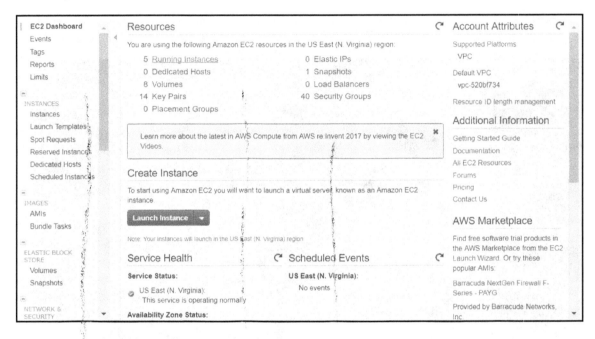

Next, we will provide names for the instances created: `marathon1`, `mesos-slave1`, `mesos-slave2`, `mesos-master1`, and `mesos-master2`.

Creating backup

What if your server goes down? To avoid that, we will create few more instances in another subnet to have high availability. This is how you can make sure your application is highly available and reliable.

Let's start by creating remaining three servers on another availability zone. This can be done by clicking on **Launch Instance**, and selecting the AMI from AWS Marketplace. This will be the same that we created earlier, which is CentOS7. Here, we will select **t2.micro** instances, just as before. We will now need three instances. Select our VPC but with another subnet that we created. We will select the **Enable auto-assign Public IP** option this time so that we'll have the auto-assigned IP address. Now we will change the **Volume Type** to **General Purpose SSD**, and rest we will keep as it is, including the **Tags** section.

In the **Configure Security Group** section, we will just allow port 22 right now, and name the group `mesos1`. Review the instance details and click on **Launch**. We will use the existing key pair, which we already have, and under **Select a key pair** we will pick our **mesos** key pair and click on **Launch Instances**. Since the instances have started, we will now go to EC2, and under **Reserved Instances** you will find the three instances we created:

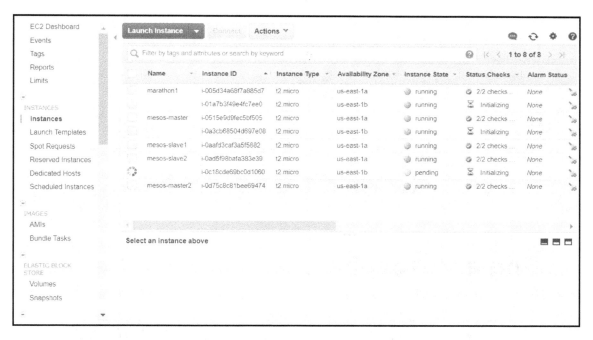

Once these instances are in the starting phase, we will name the newly-created instances `marathon2`, `mesos-master3`, and `mesos-slave3`:

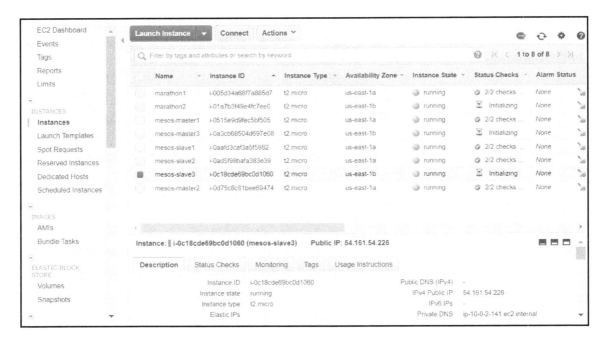

With this, we now know how we can launch the different instances on different subnets to achieve high availability. We will install components of Mesos on the EC2 instance and have used CentOS AMI to build our EC2 instance by logging in with the centos user.

Adding a Mesosphere repository in CentOS

In order to add the `mesosphere` repository, run and install a command, as shown:

```
[centos@mesos ~]$ sudo rpm -Uvh http://repos.mesosphere.io/el/7/noarch/RPMS/mesosphere-el-repo-7-1.noarch.rpm
Retrieving http://repos.mesosphere.io/el/7/noarch/RPMS/mesosphere-el-repo-7-1.noarch.rpm
Preparing...                          ################################# [100%]
Updating / installing...
   1:mesosphere-el-repo-7-1            ################################# [100%]
[centos@mesos ~]$
```

After this, install ZooKeeper with `yum` by running the `sudo yum install mesosphere-zookeeper` command. This will install ZooKeeper on CentOS:

```
[centos@mesos ~]$ sudo yum install mesosphere-zookeeper
Loaded plugins: fastestmirror
Loading mirror speeds from cached hostfile
 * base: mirrors.rit.edu
 * extras: linux.cc.lehigh.edu
 * updates: mirror.atlanticmetro.net
Resolving Dependencies
There are unfinished transactions remaining. You might consider running yum-complete-transaction, or "y
um-complete-transaction --cleanup-only" and "yum history redo last", first to finish them. If those don
't work you'll have to try removing/installing packages by hand (maybe package-cleanup can help).
--> Running transaction check
---> Package mesosphere-zookeeper.x86_64 0:3.4.6-0.1.20141204175332.centos7 will be installed
--> Finished Dependency Resolution

Dependencies Resolved

================================================================================
 Package                Arch       Version                          Repository       Size
================================================================================
Installing:
 mesosphere-zookeeper   x86_64     3.4.6-0.1.20141204175332.centos7   mesosphere      2.8 M

Transaction Summary
================================================================================
Install  1 Package

Total download size: 2.8 M
Installed size: 3.5 M
Is this ok [y/d/N]: y
```

We can see the `mesosphere-zookeeper` package with version 3.4.6 from the `mesosphere` repository, and the size is `2.8` MB.

This screenshot shows that the package has been installed:

```
Downloading packages:
mesosphere-zookeeper-3.4.6-0.1.20141204175332.centos7.x86_64.rpm              | 2.8 MB  00:00:00
Running transaction check
Running transaction test
Transaction test succeeded
Running transaction
Warning: RPMDB altered outside of yum.
  Installing : mesosphere-zookeeper-3.4.6-0.1.20141204175332.centos7.x86_64                        1/1
  Verifying  : mesosphere-zookeeper-3.4.6-0.1.20141204175332.centos7.x86_64                        1/1

Installed:
  mesosphere-zookeeper.x86_64 0:3.4.6-0.1.20141204175332.centos7

Complete!
[centos@mesos ~]$
```

Now, install the Mesos master and Mesos slave, as shown:

```
[centos@mesos ~]$ sudo yum install mesos
Loaded plugins: fastestmirror
Loading mirror speeds from cached hostfile
 * base: mirrors.rit.edu
 * extras: linux.cc.lehigh.edu
 * updates: mirror.cs.pitt.edu
Resolving Dependencies
There are unfinished transactions remaining. You might consider running yum-complete-transaction, or "y
um-complete-transaction --cleanup-only" and "yum history redo last", first to finish them. If those don
't work you'll have to try removing/installing packages by hand (maybe package-cleanup can help).
--> Running transaction check
---> Package mesos.x86_64 0:1.5.0-2.0.1 will be installed
--> Finished Dependency Resolution

Dependencies Resolved

================================================================================
 Package          Arch          Version          Repository          Size
================================================================================
Installing:
 mesos            x86_64        1.5.0-2.0.1      mesosphere          76 M

Transaction Summary
================================================================================
Install  1 Package

Total download size: 76 M
Installed size: 244 M
Is this ok [y/d/N]: y
```

We can see the `mesos` package version 1.5 from the `mesosphere` repository, and the size is 76 MB.

Hence, this will download and install Mesos, which will comprise the Mesos master and slave service, as seen here:

```
Downloading packages:
mesos-1.5.0-2.0.1.el7.x86_64.rpm                              |  76 MB  00:00:01
Running transaction check
Running transaction test
Transaction test succeeded
Running transaction
  Installing : mesos-1.5.0-2.0.1.x86_64                                      1/1
  Verifying  : mesos-1.5.0-2.0.1.x86_64                                      1/1

Installed:
  mesos.x86_64 0:1.5.0-2.0.1

Complete!
[centos@mesos ~]$
```

Installing Docker Community Edition

The `sudo yum-config-manager` command will add a Docker repository in our CentOS, as seen in the following screenshot:

```
[centos@mesos ~]$ sudo yum-config-manager --add-repo https://download.docker.com/linux/centos/docker-ce
.repo
Loaded plugins: fastestmirror
adding repo from: https://download.docker.com/linux/centos/docker-ce.repo
grabbing file https://download.docker.com/linux/centos/docker-ce.repo to /etc/yum.repos.d/docker-ce.rep
o
repo saved to /etc/yum.repos.d/docker-ce.repo
[centos@mesos ~]$
```

Run the `sudo yum install docker-ce` command:

```
[centos@mesos ~]$ sudo yum install docker -ce
```

Type `yes`, which will install Docker Community Edition:

```
Dependencies Resolved

================================================================================
 Package           Arch          Version                    Repository       Size
================================================================================
Installing:
 docker-ce         x86_64        18.03.0.ce-1.el7.centos     docker-ce-stable  35 M

Transaction Summary
================================================================================
Install  1 Package

Total download size: 35 M
Installed size: 151 M
Is this ok [y/d/N]: y
Downloading packages:
docker-ce-18.03.0.ce-1.el7.centos.x86_64.rpm              |  35 MB  00:00:00
Running transaction check
Running transaction test
Transaction test succeeded
Running transaction
  Installing : docker-ce-18.03.0.ce-1.el7.centos.x86_64               1/1
  Verifying  : docker-ce-18.03.0.ce-1.el7.centos.x86_64               1/1

Installed:
  docker-ce.x86_64 0:18.03.0.ce-1.el7.centos

Complete!
[centos@mesos ~]$
```

Configuring ZooKeeper

Perform the following steps to configure ZooKeeper:

1. Type `cd /etc /mesos`.
2. Open the `vi zk` file. The following screenshot shows the default Mesos definition. This is the default ZooKeeper information. The line starts with `zk` and ends with `/mesos`, and in between, we will have the IP address and the ZooKeeper port:

3. Replace this localhost with the host IP address by typing `ifconfig` in order to get the IP. As we have a standalone server, we will use the IP address that is highlighted here:

```
[centos@mesos mesos]$ ifconfig
docker0: flags=4099<UP,BROADCAST,MULTICAST>  mtu 1500
        inet 172.17.0.1  netmask 255.255.0.0  broadcast 172.17.255.255
        ether 02:42:73:ef:ab:38  txqueuelen 0  (Ethernet)
        RX packets 0  bytes 0 (0.0 B)
        RX errors 0  dropped 0  overruns 0  frame 0
        TX packets 0  bytes 0 (0.0 B)
        TX errors 0  dropped 0 overruns 0  carrier 0  collisions 0

eth0: flags=4163<UP,BROADCAST,RUNNING,MULTICAST>  mtu 9001
        inet 10.0.1.42  netmask 255.255.255.0  broadcast 10.0.1.255
        inet6 fe80::92:3ff:fe0d:74d8  prefixlen 64  scopeid 0x20<link>
        ether 02:92:03:0d:74:d8  txqueuelen 1000  (Ethernet)
        RX packets 215385  bytes 265091215 (252.8 MiB)
        RX errors 0  dropped 0  overruns 0  frame 0
        TX packets 100038  bytes 7227084 (6.8 MiB)
        TX errors 0  dropped 0 overruns 0  carrier 0  collisions 0

lo: flags=73<UP,LOOPBACK,RUNNING>  mtu 65536
        inet 127.0.0.1  netmask 255.0.0.0
        inet6 ::1  prefixlen 128  scopeid 0x10<host>
        loop  txqueuelen 1  (Local Loopback)
        RX packets 6  bytes 416 (416.0 B)
        RX errors 0  dropped 0  overruns 0  frame 0
        TX packets 6  bytes 416 (416.0 B)
        TX errors 0  dropped 0 overruns 0  carrier 0  collisions 0
```

4. Go to `cd /etc /mesos` and run `sudo vi zk` to replace the IP.
5. Save the file. This completes the ZooKeeper connection information for Mesos.
6. Map the unique ID by typing `var/lib/zookeeper` and `cat myid`.
7. It has defined 1. As we have a standalone system, we will keep ID 1 for this server only.

If you don't have this `myid` file, you need to create it by typing `myid`, and inside the file you can define the number 1.

8. To map the ZooKeeper ID, type `cd /etc/zookeeper/conf/` and run cat `zoo.cfg`, as shown here:

```
[centos@mesos conf]$ cat zoo.cfg
# Licensed to the Apache Software Foundation (ASF) under one or more
# contributor license agreements.  See the NOTICE file distributed with
# this work for additional information regarding copyright ownership.
# The ASF licenses this file to You under the Apache License, Version 2.0
# (the "License"); you may not use this file except in compliance with
# the License.  You may obtain a copy of the License at
#
#     http://www.apache.org/licenses/LICENSE-2.0
#
# Unless required by applicable law or agreed to in writing, software
# distributed under the License is distributed on an "AS IS" BASIS,
# WITHOUT WARRANTIES OR CONDITIONS OF ANY KIND, either express or implied.
# See the License for the specific language governing permissions and
# limitations under the License.

maxClientCnxns=50
# The number of milliseconds of each tick
tickTime=2000
# The number of ticks that the initial
# synchronization phase can take
initLimit=10
# The number of ticks that can pass between
# sending a request and getting an acknowledgement
syncLimit=5
# the directory where the snapshot is stored.
dataDir=/var/lib/zookeeper
# the port at which the clients will connect
clientPort=2181
[centos@mesos conf]$
```

9. Open the file and add this:

```
[centos@mesos conf]$ sudo vi zoo.cfg
```

```
server.1=10.0.1.42:2888:3888
```

This is required to elect the leader and to have communication. So, this step is important when your cluster environment is in your multiple nodes. We will do this as it is and save the file.

10. To configure Mesos, go inside `cd etc/mesos-master` and define your quorum hostname and IP address. The quorum setting is required to make a decision by electing a leader, but in this scenario we will keep the default what we have. So, if you see `vi quorum`, or you can do `cat quorum`, keep the setting as 1.

11. Change the IP address and hostname, check your IP address, which is `10.0.1.42`. Then type `vi hostname` and define the hostname. Check the hostname, which is `mesos`. Type `sudo vi hostname` and make sure the hostname is `mesos`.

Thus, we have completed Mesos configuration by adding the `quorum`, `ip`, and `hostname`:

```
[centos@mesos mesos-master]$ cd /etc/mesos-master/
[centos@mesos mesos-master]$ ls -rlt
total 16
-rw-rw-r--. 1 root root 15 Feb  8 16:22 work_dir
-rw-rw-r--. 1 root root  2 Feb  8 16:22 quorum
-rw-r--r--. 1 root root 10 Mar  3 06:49 ip
-rw-r--r--. 1 root root  6 Mar 28 04:55 hostname
drwxr-xr-x. 2 root root 67 Mar 28 05:00 bak
[centos@mesos mesos-master]$
```

ZooKeeper

To start ZooKeeper, type `sudo service zookeeper start`. Check the status:

```
[centos@mesos mesos-master]$ sudo service zookeeper start
Redirecting to /bin/systemctl start zookeeper.service
[centos@mesos mesos-master]$ sudo service zookeeper status
Redirecting to /bin/systemctl status zookeeper.service
● zookeeper.service - Apache ZooKeeper
   Loaded: loaded (/usr/lib/systemd/system/zookeeper.service; enabled; vendor preset: disabled)
   Active: active (running) since Wed 2018-03-28 05:05:42 UTC; 2s ago
 Main PID: 7497 (java)
   Memory: 34.7M
   CGroup: /system.slice/zookeeper.service
           └─7497 java -Dzookeeper.log.dir=. -Dzookeeper.root.logger=INFO,CONSOLE -cp /opt/mesospher...

Mar 28 05:05:43 mesos zookeeper[7497]: 2018-03-28 05:05:43,317 [myid:] - INFO  [main:Environment...md64
Mar 28 05:05:43 mesos zookeeper[7497]: 2018-03-28 05:05:43,317 [myid:] - INFO  [main:Environment...6_64
Mar 28 05:05:43 mesos zookeeper[7497]: 2018-03-28 05:05:43,317 [myid:] - INFO  [main:Environment...root
Mar 28 05:05:43 mesos zookeeper[7497]: 2018-03-28 05:05:43,317 [myid:] - INFO  [main:Environment...root
Mar 28 05:05:43 mesos zookeeper[7497]: 2018-03-28 05:05:43,317 [myid:] - INFO  [main:Environment...eper
Mar 28 05:05:43 mesos zookeeper[7497]: 2018-03-28 05:05:43,326 [myid:] - INFO  [main:ZooKeeperSe...2000
Mar 28 05:05:43 mesos zookeeper[7497]: 2018-03-28 05:05:43,326 [myid:] - INFO  [main:ZooKeeperSe...o -1
Mar 28 05:05:43 mesos zookeeper[7497]: 2018-03-28 05:05:43,328 [myid:] - INFO  [main:ZooKeeperSe...o -1
Mar 28 05:05:43 mesos zookeeper[7497]: 2018-03-28 05:05:43,340 [myid:] - INFO  [main:NIOServerCn...2181
Mar 28 05:05:43 mesos zookeeper[7497]: 2018-03-28 05:05:43,362 [myid:] - INFO  [main:FileSnap@83...00aa
Hint: Some lines were ellipsized, use -l to show in full.
```

You can see status -l has more information:

```
[centos@mesos mesos-master]$ sudo service zookeeper status -l
```

```
      └─7497 java -Dzookeeper.log.dir=. -Dzookeeper.root.logger=INFO,CONSOLE -cp /opt/mesosphere/z
ookeeper/bin/../build/classes:/opt/mesosphere/zookeeper/bin/../build/lib/*.jar:/opt/mesosphere/zookeepe
r/bin/../lib/slf4j-log4j12-1.6.1.jar:/opt/mesosphere/zookeeper/bin/../lib/slf4j-api-1.6.1.jar:/opt/meso
sphere/zookeeper/bin/../lib/netty-3.7.0.Final.jar:/opt/mesosphere/zookeeper/bin/../lib/log4j-1.2.16.jar
:/opt/mesosphere/zookeeper/bin/../lib/jline-0.9.94.jar:/opt/mesosphere/zookeeper/bin/../zookeeper-3.4.6
.jar:/opt/mesosphere/zookeeper/bin/../src/java/lib/*.jar:/etc/zookeeper/conf: -Dcom.sun.management.jmxr
emote -Dcom.sun.management.jmxremote.local.only=false org.apache.zookeeper.server.quorum.QuorumPeerMain
/etc/zookeeper/conf/zoo.cfg

Mar 28 05:05:43 mesos zookeeper[7497]: 2018-03-28 05:05:43,317 [myid:] - INFO  [main:Environment@100] -
 Server environment:os.arch=amd64
Mar 28 05:05:43 mesos zookeeper[7497]: 2018-03-28 05:05:43,317 [myid:] - INFO  [main:Environment@100] -
 Server environment:os.version=3.10.0-693.11.6.el7.x86_64
Mar 28 05:05:43 mesos zookeeper[7497]: 2018-03-28 05:05:43,317 [myid:] - INFO  [main:Environment@100] -
 Server environment:user.name=root
Mar 28 05:05:43 mesos zookeeper[7497]: 2018-03-28 05:05:43,317 [myid:] - INFO  [main:Environment@100] -
 Server environment:user.home=/root
Mar 28 05:05:43 mesos zookeeper[7497]: 2018-03-28 05:05:43,317 [myid:] - INFO  [main:Environment@100] -
 Server environment:user.dir=/opt/mesosphere/zookeeper
Mar 28 05:05:43 mesos zookeeper[7497]: 2018-03-28 05:05:43,326 [myid:] - INFO  [main:ZooKeeperServer@75
5] - tickTime set to 2000
Mar 28 05:05:43 mesos zookeeper[7497]: 2018-03-28 05:05:43,326 [myid:] - INFO  [main:ZooKeeperServer@76
4] - minSessionTimeout set to -1
Mar 28 05:05:43 mesos zookeeper[7497]: 2018-03-28 05:05:43,328 [myid:] - INFO  [main:ZooKeeperServer@77
3] - maxSessionTimeout set to -1
Mar 28 05:05:43 mesos zookeeper[7497]: 2018-03-28 05:05:43,340 [myid:] - INFO  [main:NIOServerCnxnFacto
ry@94] - binding to port 0.0.0.0/0.0.0.0:2181
Mar 28 05:05:43 mesos zookeeper[7497]: 2018-03-28 05:05:43,362 [myid:] - INFO  [main:FileSnap@83] - Rea
ding snapshot /var/lib/zookeeper/version-2/snapshot.21000000aa
[centos@mesos mesos-master]$ 
```

Run `sudo service mesos-master start`, and see the status:

```
[centos@mesos mesos-master]$ sudo service mesos-master start
Redirecting to /bin/systemctl start mesos-master.service
[centos@mesos mesos-master]$ sudo service mesos-master status
Redirecting to /bin/systemctl status mesos-master.service
● mesos-master.service - Mesos Master
   Loaded: loaded (/usr/lib/systemd/system/mesos-master.service; enabled; vendor preset: disabled)
   Active: active (running) since Wed 2018-03-28 05:06:08 UTC; 3s ago
 Main PID: 7576 (mesos-master)
   Memory: 7.0M
   CGroup: /system.slice/mesos-master.service
           ├─7576 /usr/sbin/mesos-master --zk=zk://10.0.1.42:2181/mesos --port=5050 --log_dir=/var/1...
           ├─7590 logger -p user.info -t mesos-master[7576]
           └─7591 logger -p user.err -t mesos-master[7576]

Mar 28 05:06:08 mesos mesos-master[7591]: I0328 05:06:08.446334  7596 registrar.cpp:495] Applied...stry
Mar 28 05:06:08 mesos mesos-master[7591]: I0328 05:06:08.446810  7596 coordinator.cpp:348] Coord... 661
Mar 28 05:06:08 mesos mesos-master[7591]: I0328 05:06:08.446943  7596 replica.cpp:541] Replica r...5050
Mar 28 05:06:08 mesos mesos-master[7591]: I0328 05:06:08.448894  7596 replica.cpp:695] Replica r...5050
Mar 28 05:06:08 mesos mesos-master[7591]: I0328 05:06:08.450116  7596 registrar.cpp:552] Success...92ms
Mar 28 05:06:08 mesos mesos-master[7591]: I0328 05:06:08.450194  7596 registrar.cpp:424] Success...trar
Mar 28 05:06:08 mesos mesos-master[7591]: I0328 05:06:08.450600  7596 master.cpp:1803] Recovered...ster
Mar 28 05:06:08 mesos mesos-master[7591]: I0328 05:06:08.450644  7596 coordinator.cpp:348] Coord... 662
Mar 28 05:06:08 mesos mesos-master[7591]: I0328 05:06:08.450721  7596 replica.cpp:541] Replica r...5050
Mar 28 05:06:08 mesos mesos-master[7591]: I0328 05:06:08.452381  7596 replica.cpp:695] Replica r...5050
Hint: Some lines were ellipsized, use -l to show in full.
[centos@mesos mesos-master]$
```

You can also add `-l` to get more information:

```
[centos@mesos mesos-master]$ sudo service mesos-master status -l
```

```
Mar 28 05:06:08 mesos mesos-master[7591]: I0328 05:06:08.446334  7596 registrar.cpp:495] Applied 1 oper
ations in 117568ns; attempting to update the registry
Mar 28 05:06:08 mesos mesos-master[7591]: I0328 05:06:08.446810  7596 coordinator.cpp:348] Coordinator
attempting to write APPEND action at position 661
Mar 28 05:06:08 mesos mesos-master[7591]: I0328 05:06:08.446943  7596 replica.cpp:541] Replica received
 write request for position 661 from __req_res__(2)@10.0.1.42:5050
Mar 28 05:06:08 mesos mesos-master[7591]: I0328 05:06:08.448894  7596 replica.cpp:695] Replica received
 learned notice for position 661 from log-network(1)@10.0.1.42:5050
Mar 28 05:06:08 mesos mesos-master[7591]: I0328 05:06:08.450116  7596 registrar.cpp:552] Successfully u
pdated the registry in 3.752192ms
Mar 28 05:06:08 mesos mesos-master[7591]: I0328 05:06:08.450194  7596 registrar.cpp:424] Successfully r
ecovered registrar
Mar 28 05:06:08 mesos mesos-master[7591]: I0328 05:06:08.450600  7596 master.cpp:1803] Recovered 6 agen
ts from the registry (1685B); allowing 10mins for agents to re-register
Mar 28 05:06:08 mesos mesos-master[7591]: I0328 05:06:08.450644  7596 coordinator.cpp:348] Coordinator
attempting to write TRUNCATE action at position 662
Mar 28 05:06:08 mesos mesos-master[7591]: I0328 05:06:08.450721  7596 replica.cpp:541] Replica received
 write request for position 662 from __req_res__(3)@10.0.1.42:5050
Mar 28 05:06:08 mesos mesos-master[7591]: I0328 05:06:08.452381  7596 replica.cpp:695] Replica received
 learned notice for position 662 from log-network(1)@10.0.1.42:5050
```

In order to access the console, here is the Mesos-master server and the public IP is `34.237.145.106` port is `5050`. But we won't be able to access this as we need to enable the traffic and security group.

To do so, check the **Security groups**, which is `mesos`. We need to add a rule and input `5050` as **Port Range**, in **Inbound | Edit**. Where, we will consider the source as `Anywhere` but you should define your IP or your custom IP range and save it.

Now let's go and refresh our page(`34.237.145.106:5050`). We can see that we are able to access Mesos:

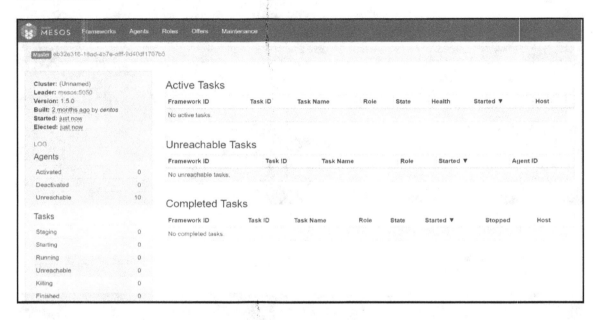

In this way, you can enable the inbound rule for your Mesos master server.

Installation of the Marathon framework

The following are the steps to install the Marathon package on the EC2 instance:

1. The following screenshot shows the Marathon server in which we will install the package and add the Mesosphere repository to install the Marathon package:

```
[centos@marathon1 ~]$ sudo rpm -Uvh http://repos.mesosphere.io/el/7/noarch/RPMS/mesosphere-el-repo-7-1.
noarch.rpm
Retrieving http://repos.mesosphere.io/el/7/noarch/RPMS/mesosphere-el-repo-7-1.noarch.rpm
Preparing...                          ################################# [100%]
Updating / installing...
   1:mesosphere-el-repo-7-1           ################################# [100%]
```

2. Install the Marathon by run the following command:

```
[centos@marathon1 ~]$ sudo yum install marathon
Loaded plugins: fastestmirror
Loading mirror speeds from cached hostfile
 * base: mirror.math.princeton.edu
 * extras: mirror.vtti.vt.edu
 * updates: centos.mirror.constant.com
Resolving Dependencies
--> Running transaction check
---> Package marathon.noarch 0:1.6.322.2bf46b341-SNAPSHOT will be installed
--> Finished Dependency Resolution

Dependencies Resolved

================================================================================
 Package        Arch        Version                    Repository          Size
================================================================================
Installing:
 marathon       noarch      1.6.322.2bf46b341-SNAPSHOT mesosphere-noarch   75 M

Transaction Summary
================================================================================
Install  1 Package

Total download size: 75 M
Installed size: 81 M
Is this ok [y/d/N]: y
Downloading packages:
systemd-marathon-1.6.322.2bf46b341-S 75% [===================-    ] 36 MB/s |  57 MB  00:00:00 ETA
```

```
Running transaction check
Running transaction test
Transaction test succeeded
Running transaction
Warning: RPMDB altered outside of yum.
Creating system group: marathon
Creating system user: marathon in marathon with marathon user-daemon and shell /bin/false
  Installing : marathon-1.6.322.2bf46b341-SNAPSHOT.noarch                     1/1
Created symlink from /etc/systemd/system/multi-user.target.wants/marathon.service to /usr/lib/systemd/s
ystem/marathon.service.
  Verifying  : marathon-1.6.322.2bf46b341-SNAPSHOT.noarch                     1/1

Installed:
  marathon.noarch 0:1.6.322.2bf46b341-SNAPSHOT

Complete!
```

3. Perform the `sudo rpm -qa | grep marathon` command, which will show the Marathon package installed:

```
[centos@marathon1 ~]$ sudo rpm -qa |grep marathon
marathon-1.6.322.2bf46b341-SNAPSHOT.noarch
[centos@marathon1 ~]$
```

Configuration of Marathon

We need to perform two configurations where we will define the Mesos master-related information and ZooKeeper information.

The following are the steps to work on the configuration of Marathon:

1. Edit the `marathon.service` file by opening the file that is inside `/etc/systemd/system/multi-user.target.wants/`. Type `ls -arlt` and you will see the `marathon.service` file:

```
[centos@marathon1 ~]$ cd /etc/systemd/system/multi-user.target.wants/
[centos@marathon1 multi-user.target.wants]$ ls -arlt
total 8
lrwxrwxrwx. 1 root root   40 Jan  8 16:27 remote-fs.target -> /usr/lib/systemd/system/remote-fs.target
lrwxrwxrwx. 1 root root   37 Jan  8 16:28 crond.service -> /usr/lib/systemd/system/crond.service
lrwxrwxrwx. 1 root root   41 Jan  8 16:28 nfs-client.target -> /usr/lib/systemd/system/nfs-client.targ
et
lrwxrwxrwx. 1 root root   44 Jan  8 16:29 cloud-config.service -> /usr/lib/systemd/system/cloud-config
.service
lrwxrwxrwx. 1 root root   43 Jan  8 16:29 cloud-final.service -> /usr/lib/systemd/system/cloud-final.s
ervice
lrwxrwxrwx. 1 root root   42 Jan  8 16:29 cloud-init.service -> /usr/lib/systemd/system/cloud-init.ser
vice
lrwxrwxrwx. 1 root root   48 Jan  8 16:29 cloud-init-local.service -> /usr/lib/systemd/system/cloud-in
it-local.service
lrwxrwxrwx. 1 root root   37 Jan  8 16:29 tuned.service -> /usr/lib/systemd/system/tuned.service
lrwxrwxrwx. 1 root root   38 Jan  8 16:29 auditd.service -> /usr/lib/systemd/system/auditd.service
lrwxrwxrwx. 1 root root   39 Jan  8 16:29 postfix.service -> /usr/lib/systemd/system/postfix.service
lrwxrwxrwx. 1 root root   42 Jan  8 16:29 irqbalance.service -> /usr/lib/systemd/system/irqbalance.ser
vice
lrwxrwxrwx. 1 root root   36 Jan  8 16:29 sshd.service -> /usr/lib/systemd/system/sshd.service
lrwxrwxrwx. 1 root root   39 Jan  8 16:29 chronyd.service -> /usr/lib/systemd/system/chronyd.service
lrwxrwxrwx. 1 root root   39 Jan  8 16:29 rsyslog.service -> /usr/lib/systemd/system/rsyslog.service
lrwxrwxrwx. 1 root root   37 Jan  8 16:32 kdump.service -> /usr/lib/systemd/system/kdump.service
drwxr-xr-x. 10 root root 4096 Jan  8 16:33 ..
lrwxrwxrwx. 1 root root   40 Apr  6 13:53 marathon.service -> /usr/lib/systemd/system/marathon.service
drwxr-xr-x. 2 root root 4096 Apr  6 13:53 .
```

2. Open that file, and you will see the basic configuration of Marathon. The language starts with `ExecStart`. Go to the end and input the master information and the ZooKeeper information. This information will help the Marathon framework to connect to Mesos master, and this information will store the Marathon information inside ZooKeeper:

```
[Unit]
Description=Scheduler for Apache Mesos
Requires=network.target

[Service]
Type=simple
WorkingDirectory=/usr/share/marathon
EnvironmentFile=/etc/default/marathon
ExecStart=/usr/share/marathon/bin/marathon --master zk://10.0.1.42:2181/mesos --zk zk://10.0.1.42:2181/
marathon
ExecReload=/bin/kill -HUP $MAINPID
Restart=always
RestartSec=60
SuccessExitStatus=
User=marathon
ExecStartPre=/bin/mkdir -p /run/marathon
ExecStartPre=/bin/chown marathon:marathon /run/marathon
ExecStartPre=/bin/chmod 755 /run/marathon
PermissionsStartOnly=true
LimitNOFILE=1024

[Install]
WantedBy=multi-user.target
```

3. Save the file, clear the screen, and do the restart. As we have edited the service file, you need to run `sudo systemctl daemon-reload`.

4. To run Marathon, check whether the JDK is installed by `java -version` command.

5. Then run `sudo service marathon start` command and check the status with `sudo service marathon start -l`. In the following screenshot, you can see that it's in the running state and it has started receiving offers as well:

```
[centos@marathon1 multi-user.target.wants]$ sudo service marathon start
Redirecting to /bin/systemctl start marathon.service
[centos@marathon1 multi-user.target.wants]$ sudo service marathon status -l
Redirecting to /bin/systemctl status -l marathon.service
● marathon.service - Scheduler for Apache Mesos
   Loaded: loaded (/usr/lib/systemd/system/marathon.service; enabled; vendor preset: disabled)
   Active: active (running) since Fri 2018-04-06 14:07:07 UTC; 1min 14s ago
  Process: 5189 ExecStartPre=/bin/chmod 755 /run/marathon (code=exited, status=0/SUCCESS)
  Process: 5186 ExecStartPre=/bin/chown marathon:marathon /run/marathon (code=exited, status=0/SUCCESS)
  Process: 5184 ExecStartPre=/bin/mkdir -p /run/marathon (code=exited, status=0/SUCCESS)
 Main PID: 5191 (java)
   CGroup: /system.slice/marathon.service
           └─5191 java -cp /usr/share/marathon/lib/mesosphere.marathon.marathon-1.6.322.jar:/usr/share/
marathon/lib/mesosphere.marathon.plugin-interface-2bf46b341ea2aac4e17ed9420cba5a9479559937.jar:/usr/sha
re/marathon/lib/org.scala-lang.scala-reflect-2.12.4.jar:/usr/share/marathon/lib/commons-codec.commons-c
odec-1.9.jar:/usr/share/marathon/lib/net.liftweb.lift-markdown_2.12-3.1.1.jar:/usr/share/marathon/lib/n
et.logstash.logback.logstash-logback-encoder-4.9.jar:/usr/share/marathon/lib/org.apache.yetus.audience-
annotations-0.5.0.jar:/usr/share/marathon/lib/io.reactivex.rxjava-1.2.4.jar:/usr/share/marathon/lib/io.
```

6. Check whether we are able to access the Marathon console. Use the hostname entries where it defined `marathon1` to the public IP in the local desktop.

7. Set the URL as `marathon1:8080`. As soon as you press *Enter*, it will bring up the landing page of Marathon, where you will see **STATUS**, **HEALTH**, and **RESOURCES**:

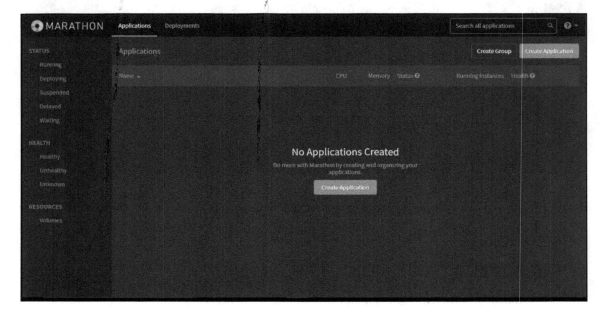

8. In the Marathon framework, create an application that will get deployed on the Mesos slave.

This concludes the setup of Marathon, the Mesos master, and the Mesos slave.

Mesos services

To check the Mesos web page, use the name on the local desktop. There will be no agent activity, so we will start our Mesos slave by typing `sudo service mesos-slave start`:

Check the status with `sudo service mesos-slave status` command. It will be in running state. Next, check the Mesos console. Click the **Agents** tab, and you will see that we have activated the agent that is running on the Mesos host. Hence, the host, CPUs, memory, and disk space are visible, which are registered:

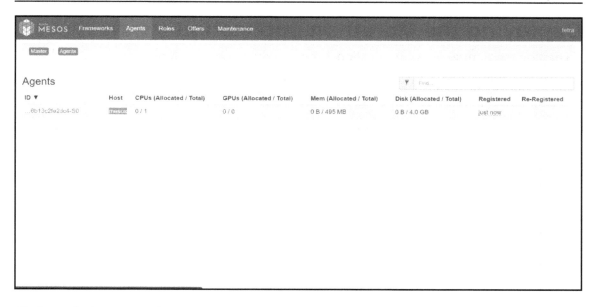

Click on the **Frameworks** tab, and then you will see which frameworks are available via the Mesos console:

Deploying the Marathon application

To deploy the sample nginx application, carry out the following steps:

1. Click on **Create Application** button. In the **General** tab, set the application ID, CPUs, memory, disk space, and **Instances,** as can be seen here:

2. In the **Docker Container** tab, type `nginx`; it will pull the latest nginx image and mark it as **Bridged**:

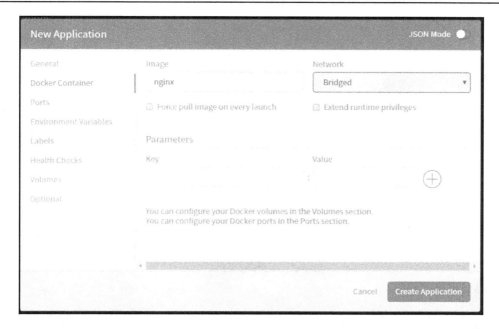

3. Enter 80 in the **Container Port** box. Type the name as nginx and click on **Create Application**. You will see how quickly our nginx image is running:

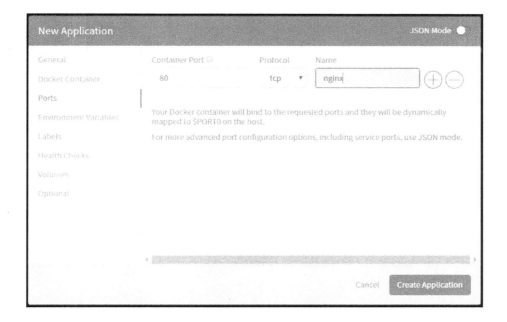

4. Click on `nginx`, which shows details for your nginx image:

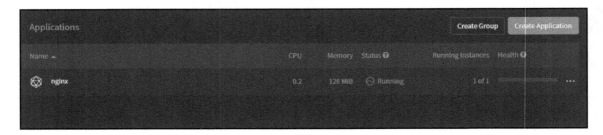

5. Click on the nginx ID, which will detail the nginx application:

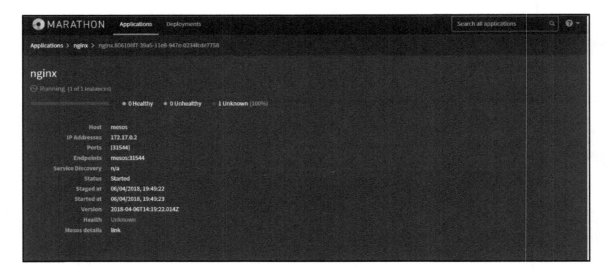

 If you click on nginx, the page won't get loaded as the security group cannot accept any port.

6. To allow the security group to accept any port in which the nginx space can be viewed, go to the **Security groups** of your EC2 instance.
7. Click on the **Inbound** tab and edit the rule.
8. Click on **Add Rule** and select **All traffic**, under **Type** field, **Anywhere** under **Source**, and then **Save**:

9. Go back to the page where our connection was refused and refresh the page; you will see the **Welcome to nginx!** page:

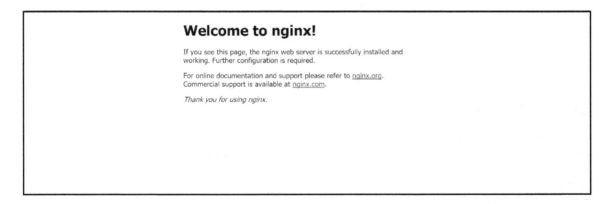

10. Check the Mesos page and you will see it has **Framework ID**, **Task ID**, and **Task Name**, and it will be in the **RUNNING** state:

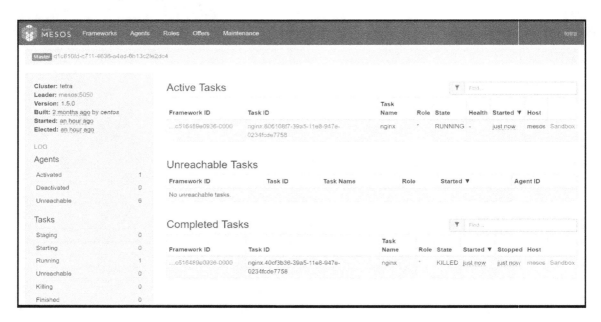

This is how you can build your development environment and deploy the application using the Marathon framework.

Summary

In this chapter, you learned how to create a VPC as well as multiple subnets in different availability zones. We also created a route table so traffic can flow between them, then we created an internet gateway to give internet access to our instances. We learned how to create an EC2 instance inside our VPC and subnet. We created multiple instances and different subnets to achieve high availability and reliability.

You also saw that you can connect to an EC2 instance in two ways: by using PuTTY, or by converting them into a PPK file and using PuTTY to connect to your instances and next using SSH. If you have Apache, you can use SSH to connect to your instances.

In the next chapter, we will see how to install Mesos and our required components on all these servers.

3
Installation of Mesosphere

In the last chapter, we worked on setting up a Mesos single-node cluster for our development environment. In this chapter, we will be extending our development environment to the production environment, meaning, we will add more components to our single-node cluster, to make our framework functional. Until now we were just focusing on how to make a single node developmental environment. Now let's see how to make this environment productive by doing some more simple configurations.

We will be covering the following topics in this chapter:

- Setting up a multi-node Mesos cluster
- Configuring a mesos-master
- Configuring Marathon
- Adding slaves

Outlining goals

Until now, we have looked at a very basic architecture, featuring just one master server and one Marathon server, which, together, form our development environment. But now, as we have to develop a production environment, we will have to add more components. Accordingly, our plan of action includes the following:

- Adding one Marathon server
- Adding two more master servers
- Adding three slave servers

This will cause our architecture to look like the following:

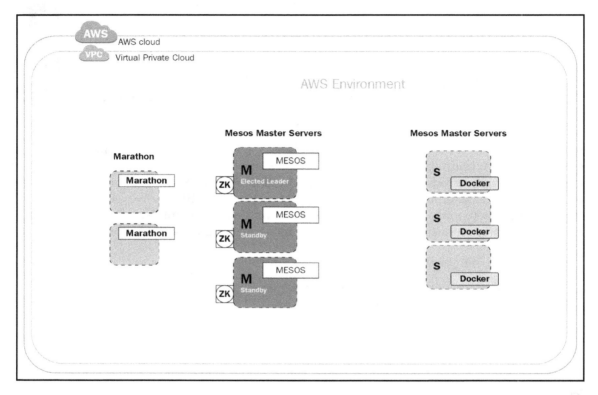

The packages that we will need to install on each of the components should be evident from the architecture shown in the above diagram. For Marathon servers, we will need to install the Marathon package; for Masters, we will install ZooKeeper; and on the slaves, we will install Docker, which is a container that will enable our applications to run. This is how we will be distributing our package installation to make a multi-node cluster. In this chapter, we won't talk in details about these packages; instead, we will focus on creating and removing nodes from the cluster. We will, however, touch upon the installation of the mesos-master and slave, ZooKeeper, Marathon, and Docker.

Setting up the framework

This section will give you insights on how to set up a multi-node cluster.

We already have Marathon and master servers ready, but they are in our development environment. So, we will change some configurations, and then extend them to production! Further, we will be including more servers as well, as described in the architecture diagram in the previous section.

The steps to install the necessary packages are as follows:

1. Add the Mesos repository with the following command:

```
rpm -Uvh
http://repos.mesosphere.io/el/7/noarch/RPMS/mesosphere-el-repo-7-1.
noarch.rpm
```

   This needs to be run on both mesos-master and slave servers.

2. After this, we can install mesos as follows:

```
sudo yum install mesos
```

   On the master server, this will install both master and slave services, but we will stop the slave services from running on all three master servers. Run this installation command on both master and slave servers.

3. To stop Mesos slave services running on master servers, enter the following command on the master tab:

```
sudo service mesos-slave stop
```

4. Then, install the ZooKeeper on master servers as follows:

```
sudo yum install mesosphere-zookeeper
```

   Ensure you run this command only on master servers.

5. Disable master services on slave servers:

```
sudo systemctl disable mesos-slave
```

6. Next, install docker on slave servers, as follows:

```
sudo yum-config-manager --add-repo
https://download.docker.com/linux/centos/docker-ce.repo
```

7. Start the docker service with this command:

```
sudo service docker start
```

8. Lastly, install `marathon` on our Marathon servers as follows:

```
sudo yum install marathon
```

This concludes our quick walkthrough of installing the necessary packages on our servers, as per their roles. You can find more detail on this in *Mesos Administration* section.

Let's now move on to the core topic of this chapter, which is configuring our mesos-master.

Configuring the mesos-master servers

After installation, configuration is a particularly important step, as it forms the basis of the whole Mesos environment.

Following are the steps to follow to configure the mesos-master:

1. First, let's set up connection information for ZooKeeper with these commands:

```
cd /etc/mesos
ls -rlt
cat zk
```

In the development environment, we had only added one mesos-master. We now need more master services, so let's add them. First, open the following file:

```
sudo vi zk
```

Now, edit the file by deleting the current entry, and inserting `zk://10.0.1.42:2181,10.0..1.203,10.0.2.68:2181/mesos`. So, basically, we have added the IP addresses of all three servers, followed by their active ports.

Save your changes and exit the file using `:wq!`. Repeat this step for all other master servers.

2. Next, let's perform our ZooKeeper configuration for the master servers. In the following steps, we will first map the unique ID on all the master servers for ZooKeeper. Then, we will define those unique IDs into `.cfg`, which is going to map unique IDs to actual hosts.

3. Define a unique ID for master1:

```
cd var/lib/zookeeper/
cat myid
//define it as 1, followed by 2 and 3 for all masters.
```

Repeat this for all master servers.

4. Map the unique IDs as follows:

```
cd /etc/zookeeper/conf
sudo vi zoo.cfg
```

5. Insert the following addresses:

```
Server.1 10.0.1.42:2888:3888
Server.2 10.0.1.203:2888:3888
Server.3 10.0.2.68:2888:3888
```

As evident, we have the unique IDs of the servers, followed by their IP addresses, and the two ports. The first port will be used for communicating with the leader, and the second one will be used to elect the leader.

Make these additions on all the master servers.

6. Set up `quorum`, which decides how many servers need to run at a time:

```
cd /etc/mesos-master/
cat quorum
//You will see a default value as 1, we will change this to 2
sudo vi quorum
//edit the value as 2, save and exit using :wq!
```

7. Now, check the IP, hostname, and cluster file as follows:

```
cat ip
//you will see an ip address
cat hostname
// and the defined hostnames
sudo touch cluster
sudo vi cluster
//Insert the name as tetra
cat cluster
//you will see the cluster name as tetra
```

8. All three files must be present on all the master servers. Validate this using the following command:

```
sudo vi /etc/hosts
//you will see all the hosts listed that will be communicating with
each other internally
```

9. Now, restart all the services:

```
sudo service zookeeper stop
sudo service mesos-master stop
ps -ef |grep mesos //No mesos service will be running
sudo service zookeeper start
sudo service zookeeper status
sudo service mesos-master start
sudo service mesos-master status // to view the status in more
detail,append -l
//Repeat the same for all the servers
```

10. Now, let's start the mesos-master services using the following commands:

```
sudo service mesos-master start
sudo service mesos-master status
```

You can see that a new master has become a candidate for leadership:

```
marathon1  marathon2  master1  master2  master3  slave1  slave2  slave3                                                    ▾

Main PID: 1509 (mesos-master)
   CGroup: /system.slice/mesos-master.service
          ├─1509 /usr/sbin/mesos-master --zk=zk://10.0.1.42:2181,10.0.1.203:2181,10.0.2.68:2181/mesos
--port=5050 --log_dir=/var/log/mesos --cluster=tetra --hostname=mesos-master3 --ip=10.0.2.68 --quorum=2
--work_dir=/var/lib/mesos
          ├─1525 logger -p user.info -t mesos-master[1509]
          └─1526 logger -p user.err -t mesos-master[1509]

Apr 07 08:10:11 mesos-master3 mesos-master[1526]: I0407 08:10:11.622368  1534 group.cpp:700] Trying to
get '/mesos/log_replicas/0000000178' in ZooKeeper
Apr 07 08:10:11 mesos-master3 mesos-master[1526]: I0407 08:10:11.622705  1533 zookeeper.cpp:262] A new
leading master (UPID=master@10.0.1.42:5050) is detected
Apr 07 08:10:11 mesos-master3 mesos-master[1526]: I0407 08:10:11.622763  1533 master.cpp:2223] The newl
y elected leader is master@10.0.1.42:5050 with id 5ee74673-e868-44c9-b057-126fdcf95852
Apr 07 08:10:11 mesos-master3 mesos-master[1526]: I0407 08:10:11.623827  1534 network.hpp:484] ZooKeepe
r group PIDs: { log-replica(1)@10.0.1.42:5050, log-replica(1)@10.0.1.203:5050 }
Apr 07 08:10:11 mesos-master3 mesos-master[1526]: I0407 08:10:11.627089  1534 network.hpp:436] ZooKeepe
r group memberships changed
Apr 07 08:10:11 mesos-master3 mesos-master[1526]: I0407 08:10:11.627138  1534 group.cpp:700] Trying to
get '/mesos/log_replicas/0000000177' in ZooKeeper
Apr 07 08:10:11 mesos-master3 mesos-master[1526]: I0407 08:10:11.627307  1529 contender.cpp:268]
Apr 07 08:10:11 mesos-master3 mesos-master[1526]: I0407 08:10:11.628298  1534 group.cpp:700] Trying to
get '/mesos/log_replicas/0000000178' in ZooKeeper
Apr 07 08:10:11 mesos-master3 mesos-master[1526]: I0407 08:10:11.629273  1534 group.cpp:700] Trying to
get '/mesos/log_replicas/0000000179' in ZooKeeper
Apr 07 08:10:11 mesos-master3 mesos-master[1526]: I0407 08:10:11.630460  1534 network.hpp:484] ZooKeepe
r group PIDs: { log-replica(1)@10.0.1.42:5050, log-replica(1)@10.0.1.203:5050, log-replica(1)@10.0.2.68
:5050 }
```

When any of the servers go down, the ZooKeeper elects a new master for leadership.

11. Now, let's access our configuration through the Mesos web page:

    Hopefully, you have defined your DNS name in hostentries. Let's check if it is running—in the address bar, type `mesos:5050`:

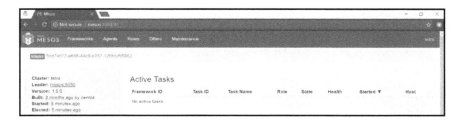

    As evident, the elected server is master1 and cluster name is tetra. Carry out checks in the same manner for master2 and master3.

    Now, let's experiment a little! Let's stop the master1 server and observe the result in the following steps.

12. We have covered how to stop the `mesos-master` service previously in this section. Perform the necessary steps on master1 and you will get the `mesos-master2:5050` as **Leader.**

You can now see that in the absence of the earlier elected leader, the ZooKeeper elected another running server as leader.

We have now extended our development environment to our host environment. Next, let's move on to configuring Marathon.

Configuring Marathon

To configure Marathon, first, we need to stop the Marathon service running on marathon1. Once this is done, we can then proceed with the following steps:

1. Go to `systemd` directory with the following command:

```
cd /etc/systemd/system/multi-user.target.wants/
```

Here, you will see the Marathon service. Type `sudo vi marathon.service` and you will see that we have added one server for our development environment, but here we need to add two more servers so that Marathon can connect with the mesos-master and deploy the applications. By adding a master configuration, our Marathon will get registered in the `mesos-master` cluster. So, let's go ahead and add two more servers in this configuration in the following steps.

2. Make the following changes in the file that we opened in the previous step:

```
ExecStart=/usr/share/marathon/bin/marathon --master
zk://10.0.1.42:2181,10.0.1.203:2181,10.0.2.68:2181/mesos --
zk://10.0.1.42:2181,10.0.1.203:2181,10.0.2.68:2181/marathon --
hostname=10.0.1.191
```

3. Run the system `daemon-reload` command and start the Marathon service, as follows:

```
sudo systemct1 daemon-reload
sudo service marathon start
sudo service marathon status
```

Wait until it gets started. You will see the following once its starts:

Then, repeat the same for marathon2.

4. Check the Marathon web console: in any browser, open two tabs and type `marathon1:8080` and `marathon2:8080` into the address bar of the respective tabs, then press *Enter*.

   This indicates that the Marathon service is up and running:

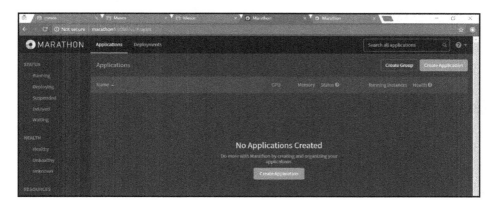

Look back to the Mesos console, and in the framework, you should see marathon1 listed:

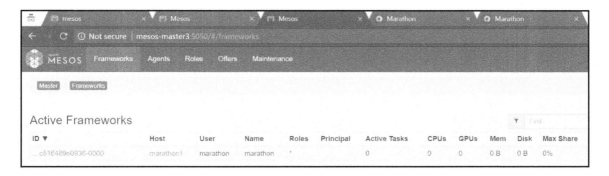

But why are we not seeing marathon2 here? You are never going to see two marathons running together. To make this clearer, let's look at what high availability and resilience are.

High availability and resilience

This is a desirable Marathon feature: when one of the Marathon servers stop, another Marathon server takes over and makes up for the loss to keep the processes running.

To see the magic happen, you will first need to stop the marathon1 service—we have covered how to stop a service previously in this chapter while configuring the mesos-master. Once this is done, go to the Mesos console, and check the difference.

Hence, we have now seen how components support each other in an architecture.

Adding slaves

Now, it is time to add the slaves to our configuration to complete our master-slave setup.

To do so, follow these simple steps:

1. Start the `docker` service on all slaves with these commands:

    ```
    sudo service docker start
    sudo service docker status
    ```

2. Start the slave services, but first, there are a few things to consider. We should have a Marathon user here:

    ```
    id marathon //include this on all 3 servers
    ```

    We need to add a Marathon user; otherwise, your application will not get deployed, so the Marathon user should be there on all the three services.

3. Change the directory to `/etc/mesos-slave`, and then, once in this directory, type `ls -rlt`. You should see the files with containerizers. Run `cat containerizer`, and you should see the two files for Mesos and Docker.

    This information should be available on all the three servers. Now we can start the slave services as follows:

    ```
    sudo service mesos-slave start
    sudo service mesos-slave status //repeat on all slaves
    ```

4. Now that the slave servers have been started, return to the Mesos console in the browser, and you can see the activated slaves:

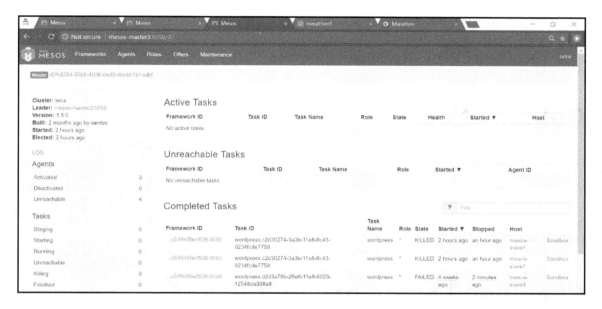

This indicates that we have successfully added slaves to our environment.

This is how we set up a multi-node Mesos cluster.

Mesos administration

We learned how to build servers on AWS. We built eight servers: two for Marathon, three for mesos-master, and three for mesos-masters and slaves in different availability zones. Remember our AWS environment diagram from Chapter 2, *Setting up Mesos Single-Cluster Nodes*? We built servers and EC2 instances for deploying our Mesos software.

In this section, we will learn how to do a basic Mesos setup containing masters and slaves. We will see which container we are going to use to enable or applications to run. We will also look in to a central mechanism, that stores the configuration files, the zookeeper.

The following are the topics that we will be covering:hostname on centos

- Installing Mesos (mesos-master and Mesos Slave)
- Installing ZooKeeper
- Installing Marathon
- Installing the Docker Container Platform

Getting started

Let's start by installing Mesosphere and its components on our AWS server. Firstly, log in to your AWS server.

You should see your internal IP address. To log in, you can use a public IP, and then, when an instance is generated, a public IP will be assigned automatically. We can now move ahead to installing the master server, but first, we need to change the hostname. The next section will tell you how this can be done.

Changing hostnames on CentOS

To successfully install Mesos, we need to change the hostname for all of the components, as we want them all to have unique and simple hostnames, so they can seamlessly interact with each other and the system. This is similar to using DNS names instead of IP addresses. Hostnames of components are generally a combination of IP addresses and paths to EC2 servers. So, let's see how we can make simpler hostnames.

After logging in to AWS, go on to the `master1` tab. We will check our current hostname, before moving on to changing it. To get started, run the following command:

```
sudo hostname ctl
```

Subsequently, you will see your current `hostname`, which will be a combination of your internal IP address and EC2 paths.

To change the `hostname`, just key in the following command:

```
sudo hostnamectl set-hostname --static mesos-master1
```

Here, `mesos-master1` is the name that we have assigned to our host—but you can assign any name you wish. Also, a small point to note here is that if you don't run this command using `sudo`, you will be asked for authentication.

After this, you will have to change your `cloud.cfg` file as per the following command:

`sudo vi /etc/cloud/cloud.cfg`

After opening the file with the preceding command, define a parameter at the end as follows:

`preserve_hostname:true`

Then save and exit using `:wq!`.

Now let's verify that we have successfully changed the `hostname`. For this, you will first have to disconnect and log in again:

1. Disconnect master 1
2. Open it again and log in

Repeat this process for all the servers: `master1`, `master2`, and `master3`. and the agents of `slave1`, `slave2`, `slave3`. Lastly, do the same for both the marathon servers.

Now let's move on to establishing communication between them.

Establishing communication

We have just changed the hostnames for all the components—now, we need to enable interaction between them. To do this, we will update the host entries on all the servers so that they can communicate with each other. So, basically, we will be communicating with our servers using DNS names, instead of IP addresses!

Here are some simple steps to follow to make the host entries. Go on to any of the servers and enter the following command:

`sudo vi /etc/hosts`

You should get a blank hosts file. Make the following entries to this file:

```
master1  master2  master3  slave1  slave2  slave3  marathon1  marathon2
127.0.0.1       localhost localhost.localdomain localhost4 localhost4.localdomain
::1             localhost localhost.localdomain localhost6 localhost6.localdomain
10.0.1.42       mesos-master1
10.0.1.203      mesos-master2
10.0.2.123      mesos-master3
10.0.1.85       mesos-slave1
10.0.1.174      mesos-slave2
10.0.2.141      mesos-slave3
10.0.1.191      marathon1
10.0.2.97       marathon2
```

Do this for all the masters, as well as for the two marathons, taking care of the internal IPs.

With this done, we can now move on to installation.

Installing Mesos

So, we are all set and ready to get into the core part of the chapter: installing Mesos.

The following section will guide you through exactly how to do this:

1. To install Mesos, we will first need to add the Mesosphere repository to all our hosts. To do this, start with master1 and use the following path:

   ```
   sudo rpm -Uvh
   http://repos.mesosphere.io/el/7/noarch/RPMS/mesosphere-el-repo-7-1.
   noarch.rpm
   ```

   This will automatically download and install the Mesosphere repository. Repeat this step for `master2`, `master3`, as well as on the slaves and marathons. With that, we are done adding repositories.

2. We can validate the addition of repositories by running the following command:

   ```
   cd /etc/yum.repos.d
   ls -rlt
   ```

You can see that the Mesosphere repository was added in the following screenshot:

```
master1 | master2 | master3 | slave1 | slave2 | slave3 | marathon1 | marathon2
[centos@mesos-master1 ~]$ sudo rpm -Uvh http://repos.mesosphere.io/el/7/noarc
/RPMS/mesosphere-el-repo-7-1.noarch.rpm
Retrieving http://repos.mesosphere.io/el/7/noarch/RPMS/mesosphere-el-repo-7-1
noarch.rpm
warning: /var/tmp/rpm-tmp.JcemM4: Header V4 RSA/SHA1 Signature, key ID e56151
f: NOKEY
Preparing...                          ################################# [100%
Updating / installing...
   1:mesosphere-el-repo-7-1            ################################# [100%
[centos@mesos-master1 ~]$ cd /etc/yum.repos.d
[centos@mesos-master1 yum.repos.d]$ ls -rlt
total 32
-rw-r--r--. 1 root root  570 Nov 13  2014 mesosphere.repo
-rw-r--r--. 1 root root 3830 Aug 30 15:53 CentOS-Vault.repo
-rw-r--r--. 1 root root 1331 Aug 30 15:53 CentOS-Sources.repo
-rw-r--r--. 1 root root  630 Aug 30 15:53 CentOS-Media.repo
-rw-r--r--. 1 root root  314 Aug 30 15:53 CentOS-fasttrack.repo
-rw-r--r--. 1 root root  649 Aug 30 15:53 CentOS-Debuginfo.repo
-rw-r--r--. 1 root root 1309 Aug 30 15:53 CentOS-CR.repo
-rw-r--r--. 1 root root 1664 Aug 30 15:53 CentOS-Base.repo
```

3. To install Mesos, return back to the `master` directory using `cd`, and then run the following command:

```
sudo yum install mesos
```

You will see that Mesosphere has checked all of its dependencies.

4. We want to install Mesos version 1.5.0 from the Mesosphere repository, so let's enter `Y` for yes, and let the installation proceed.

5. It is always good to validate whatever we do, so let's use the following command:

```
service mesos-master status
```

If your installation was successful, the following should be displayed:

```
master1   master2   master3   slave1   slave2   slave3   marathon1   marathon2

perl-Text-ParseWords.noarch 0:3.29-4.el7
perl-Time-HiRes.x86_64 4:1.9725-3.el7
perl-Time-Local.noarch 0:1.2300-2.el7
perl-constant.noarch 0:1.27-2.el7
perl-libs.x86_64 4:5.16.3-292.el7
perl-macros.x86_64 4:5.16.3-292.el7
perl-parent.noarch 1:0.225-244.el7
perl-podlators.noarch 0:2.5.1-3.el7
perl-threads.x86_64 0:1.87-4.el7
perl-threads-shared.x86_64 0:1.43-6.el7
subversion.x86_64 0:1.7.14-11.el7_4
subversion-libs.x86_64 0:1.7.14-11.el7_4
trousers.x86_64 0:0.3.14-2.el7

Complete!
[centos@mesos-master1 ~]$ service mesos-master status
Redirecting to /bin/systemctl status mesos-master.service
● mesos-master.service - Mesos Master
   Loaded: loaded (/usr/lib/systemd/system/mesos-master.service; enabled; ven
or preset: disabled)
   Active: inactive (dead)
[centos@mesos-master1 ~]$
```

Do you see the inactive state? Well, fear not. It is just a contradiction—this actually indicates that we have successfully installed Mesos! It is just that the services haven't started yet. But hold on—we won't start any services just yet. Let's first start installing Mesos similarly across all the servers. Once you're done, let's move on to installing ZooKeeper in the next section.

Installing ZooKeeper

ZooKeeper provides centralized services for distributed systems. It maintains a central repository for its configuration files. The clients and the servers on the distributed system can access these files and run their processes smoothly.

Let's see how we can install ZooKeeper in our Mesos framework:

1. Run this command to install ZooKeeper:

   ```
   sudo yum install mesosphere-zookeeper
   ```

2. You will see that the ZooKeeper package is found. We will be installing the ZooKeeper version 3.4.6. Enter Y for yes.

This will automatically install all the dependencies that ZooKeeper requires to run. Simple, isn't it?

3. After all the packages are downloaded, you should see the following:

```
master1 / master2 / master3 / slave1 / slave2 / slave3 / marathon1 / marat
libXcomposite.x86_64 0:0.4.4-4.1.el7
libXext.x86_64 0:1.3.3-3.el7
libXfont.x86_64 0:1.5.2-1.el7
libXi.x86_64 0:1.7.9-1.el7
libXrender.x86_64 0:0.9.10-1.el7
libXtst.x86_64 0:1.2.3-1.el7
libfontenc.x86_64 0:1.1.3-3.el7
libjpeg-turbo.x86_64 0:1.2.90-5.el7
libpng.x86_64 2:1.5.13-7.el7_2
libxcb.x86_64 0:1.12-1.el7
libxslt.x86_64 0:1.1.28-5.el7
lksctp-tools.x86_64 0:1.0.17-2.el7
python-javapackages.noarch 0:3.4.1-11.el7
python-lxml.x86_64 0:3.2.1-4.el7
stix-fonts.noarch 0:1.1.0-5.el7
ttmkfdir.x86_64 0:3.0.9-42.el7
tzdata-java.noarch 0:2018c-1.el7
xorg-x11-font-utils.x86_64 1:7.5-20.el7
xorg-x11-fonts-Type1.noarch 0:7.5-9.el7

Complete!
```

4. Let's now check the ZooKeeper services with the following command:

```
service zookeeper status
```

You will again see the status as inactive, but this is nothing to worry about—we will be starting the services later, after performing all the configurations.

To continue, install ZooKeeper on all the masters. We won't bother installing ZooKeeper on slaves, as when we install it for the master, it gets installed for slaves automatically.

To save time, you can use the `history` command to grab previous commands used, and then paste them on other servers.
You can also run the install command as `sudo yum -y install mesos`, which will eliminate the need to say yes every time the process is set to ask. With this command, it will automatically consider those instances as agreed to, and continue the installation without needing your intervention.

You will notice that installation will be simple for the servers, as we added the repository previously. And with that, we have now installed the masters and slaves. Let's now move on to installing Marathon.

Installing Marathon

Marathon is similar to traditional `init` systems. Here, for Mesos, it is a that helps in launching long applications.

Go to the **Marathon** tab. We can install it by running the following command:

```
sudo yum -y install marathon
```

And that's it, we are done with installing marathon. Perform this for the other server as well.

You can see the status as `FAILURE`, which is a good sign, remember? We will start the services later on:

```
master1   master2   master3   slave1   slave2   slave3   marathon1   marathon2

[centos@marathon2 yum.repos.d]$ service marathon status
Redirecting to /bin/systemctl status marathon.service
● marathon.service - Scheduler for Apache Mesos
   Loaded: loaded (/usr/lib/systemd/system/marathon.service; enabled; vendor
reset: disabled)
   Active: activating (auto-restart) (Result: exit-code) since Tue 2018-02-27
17:46:00 UTC; 9s ago
  Process: 8760 ExecStart=/usr/share/marathon/bin/marathon (code=exited, stat
us=1/FAILURE)
  Process: 8757 ExecStartPre=/bin/chmod 755 /run/marathon (code=exited, statu
=0/SUCCESS)
  Process: 8753 ExecStartPre=/bin/chown marathon:marathon /run/marathon (code
exited, status=0/SUCCESS)
  Process: 8751 ExecStartPre=/bin/mkdir -p /run/marathon (code=exited, status
0/SUCCESS)
 Main PID: 8760 (code=exited, status=1/FAILURE)

Feb 27 17:46:00 marathon2 systemd[1]: marathon.service: main process exite...
Feb 27 17:46:00 marathon2 systemd[1]: Unit marathon.service entered failed...
Feb 27 17:46:00 marathon2 systemd[1]: marathon.service failed.
Hint: Some lines were ellipsized, use -l to show in full.
```

Validating services

Let's now validate everything we have done up until now by testing if all the services are running.

To validate our masters, go to a master's tab and enter the following command:

```
sudo service mesos-master start
```

Then, to check the status, run the following command:

```
sudo service mesos-master status
```

You will now see what you have been waiting for:

Did you forget the ZooKeeper yet? Let's check that too. First, we start the service with the following command:

```
sudo service zookeeper start
```

Then, to check its status, run the following:

```
sudo service zookeeper status
```

You should see a similar active status to that shown in the preceding screenshot.

To validate slaves, run the following command on a slave's tab:

```
sudo service mesos-slave start
```

Then, to check the status, run the following command:

```
sudo service mesos-slave status
```

Marathon needs some more configuration first, so we will start its services later. We have installed Mesos for masters and slaves.

Installing Docker

All of our applications require containers to run, so we will use a Docker container to enable them to run.

These are few steps that will help us do that:

1. Add the Docker repository as follows:

    ```
    sudo yum- config-manager --add-repo
    https://download.docker.com/linux/centos/docker-ce.repo
    ```

    You can see the path to where the Docker repository is saved, as follows:

2. Install Docker with the following command (we're using the Community Edition of Docker here):

    ```
    sudo yum install docker-ce
    ```

    We are installing Docker version 17.12.0. We have now installed the Docker containers—repeat the same steps for slave2 and slave3.

3. Next, start the service with the following command:

    ```
    sudo service docker start
    ```

4. Now let's check the status:

    ```
    sudo service docker status
    ```

    You can also check the Docker information with this command:

    ```
    sudo service docker info
    ```

And, with that, Docker is now ready for our applications to use. This will be managed by our Apache Mesosphere.

Summary

In this chapter, we learned how to change the hostname on CentOS, before starting with our installations. We then installed Mesos on our three master servers, and we installed slaves on all three slave servers. We added the Mesosphere repository, and then installed Mesos. Following that, we installed ZooKeeper on all our master servers, along with installing Marathon and Docker. We also saw how you can quickly start and stop the Mesosphere services and validate their status.

We also studied how to set up a multi-node Mesos cluster. We revised the package installation for respective servers and learned how to configure a mesos-master and Marathon server, and also adding slaves. So, basically, we are now well-equipped with the knowledge of setting up a muti-cluster mesos environment.

In the next chapter, we will learn about Mesos administration in detail by understanding how to schedule and allocate resources, along with an understanding of fault tolerance and high availability.

Apache Mesos Administration

4

In the last chapter, we learned how to set up a Mesos cluster in a multi-node environment. In this chapter, we will learn about different Mesos Administrative work.

In this chapter, we will learn about the following topics:

- Scheduling and allocating resources
- Understanding fault tolerance and high availability
- Configuring ZooKeeper connection information for Mesos
- ZooKeeper configuration setup on master servers
- Mesos configuration on master servers
- Configuring marathon services
- Allowing communication between subnets in AWS
- Allowing inbound access to Mesos and Marathon consoles in AWS
- Testing high availability for Mesos and Marathon services
- Starting mesos-slave and registering in Mesos Cluster

Scheduling and allocating resources

In section, we will understand

Understanding resource scheduling

Mesos has two levels of resource scheduling, which are as follows:

- In the first level, the Mesos master process gets the details of the free resources available on each node from the slave process. From there the master process gets the details of the free resources, such as CPU, memory, and so on, that are available on each slave process. Then, it groups them and offers them with a different framework, such as Marathon, Cassandra, or any of the other available frameworks available to the Mesos cluster.
- In the second level, frameworks registered as a client with the master accept or reject the offer, depending upon the requirements.
- If the offer is accepted, the framework sends the details regarding tasks and the number of each task required to the Mesos master, and then the master transfers the request to the Mesos slave to launch those tasks on nodes, and assigns required resources to the task. So, if the offer is accepted, the framework sends the details regarding tasks, such as the application, or any Docker container which it wants to run on the Mesos slave. The Mesos master gets the details from the framework, and in turn, Mesos transfers these requests to the Mesos slave to launch those tasks on a node, and assigns the required resources to the task.
- For example, the framework accepts the offer of 2 CPUs and 4 GB RAM. The Mesos master understands that offer, and looks to the Mesos slave for where the resources may be available, and allocates that application to the node wherever the resources are available. Then, the Mesos slave launches the task on nodes, and assigns the required resources to the task.
- After assigning the task, the slave manages the execution of tasks, and when the tasks are completed, the resources are freed and handed back to the Mesos master for further assignments.

Understanding resource allocation

Let's understand the resource location as follows:

- The Mesos master uses the resource allocation module to determine the type and quantity of resource offers to be made to frameworks.
- Resource allocation modules are responsible for providing shared resources in a fair manner to competing frameworks.
- Mesos has the **dominant resource fairness** (DRF) algorithm as its default resource allocation policy, which is far more suitable for most environments.

- So, let's consider a case where the total resources available are 8 CPUs and 10 GB of memory. User 1 runs tasks that require 1 CPU and 3 GB of memory, and user 2 runs tasks that require 3 CPUs and 1 GB of memory. Let's understand the following concepts:

  - Dominant resource refers to the resources, which are CPUs and memory, that are most required by the user. In this case, user 1 runs tasks that have higher memory requirements of 3 GB per task, so the dominant resource for user 1 is memory. On the other hand, user 2 runs computation-heavy tasks using 3 CPUs per task, and hence the CPU is its dominant resource.

  - In dominant share, the master calculates the dominant share and how it will distribute the resources by referring to the fraction of the dominant resource that the user is allocated. Referring to our example, user 1's dominant share becomes 30 percent, which is 3/10, whereas user 2's dominant share is 37.5 percent, which is 3/8. This is how Mesos manages resource allocation to all the tasks given by the framework.

Let's take a look at the following screenshot:

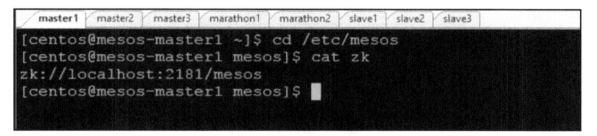

Framework 1 schedules job 1 and job 2 and the Mesos master, which has the allocation module and slave 1 and slave 2 nodes, which runs our task. The task is scheduled by the framework and managed by our Mesos master. As soon as the slave has the process of Mesos slave, the process starts. It registers the available CPU and memory to the Mesos master, which is 4 CPUs and 4 GB RAM. Then, the Mesos master offers that CPU and memory to the framework. Now, the Mesos master knows that slave 1 has 4 CPUs and 4 GB RAM. If any job requires CPU and memory, the Mesos master analyzes how much CPU and memory is required by job 1.

In our case, if we look at task 1, we can see that it asked for 2 CPUs and 1 GB RAM. The Mesos master runs job 1 on slave 1, and then job 1 is executed on slave 1. If job 2 needs to be scheduled, which requires 1 CPU and 2 GB RAM, it again goes to slave1, because it has 2 CPUs and 3 GB RAM remaining, and task 2 requires 1 CPU and 2 GB of memory. So, it again schedules that task to slave 1. This is how the Mesos master allocates and schedules the resources.

Now, in this case, slave 1 has had its resources fully allocated and executes the task. If any new task needs to be run, the Mesos master checks if it has any available resources from any other slave, and as soon as any framework requests any job to be run, the Mesos master runs that job on the node where the resources are available.

Let's understand this by visiting our Mesos cluster UI:

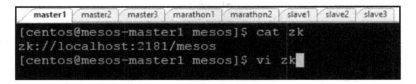

We can observe that we don't have the necessary resources here, as all the slave nodes are in a shutdown state. We will see how our two-level scheduling works here. First, we will start the slave server and see how the slave informs the master about the resources. So, let's go ahead and start one of the slave servers.

Start slave1 and check its status as follows:

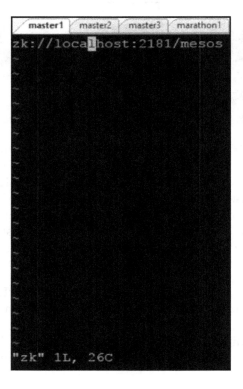

As you can see, it hasn't started. To check this, run the following command:

Then, you will see the slave logs:

Check the error log—it's giving a Docker error.

First let's start Docker:

```
[centos@mesos-master1 mesos]$ cat zk
zk://localhost:2181/mesos
[centos@mesos-master1 mesos]$ vi zk
[centos@mesos-master1 mesos]$
```

We can see that, as soon as we start Docker, our slave will go into a running state. Let's quickly go to our console and validate this:

In the console, the activated agent is 1, so it has a reported total of 1 CPU and 495 MB of memory, and 4 GB disk space. If you go to Agents, you will see that `mesos-slave1` has been registered. Now, start the other two agents as well.

After starting Docker and the slaves, check the console:

In our console, we can see that the other two slaves are registered, and it has reported the resources as 3 CPUs, 1.5 GB RAM, and 12 GB of hard disk space. During the first level, all the of slave resources report the resources to the Mesos master, so the Mesos master gathers all of the necessary steps and gives you the information together, which says 3 CPU, 1.5 GB RAM, and 12 GB of disk space. So, in the second level, all offers go to the framework. Our framework is Marathon.

Let's create one of the applications, called **nginx**. Our CPUs will be set to 0.5, and our disk image is 200. In the Docker container, the image will be nginx. The network will be set to Bridged. In the **Ports** section, the container port is 80 and the name will be nginx. Then, click on **Create Application**. Here you can see that the status deploys and then runs:

The status has been sent to Mesos slave 2. Let's quickly check our Mesos console:

```
master1   master2   master3   marathon1   marathon2   slave1   slave2   slave3

[centos@mesos-master1 mesos]$ cat zk
zk://localhost:2181/mesos
[centos@mesos-master1 mesos]$ sudo vi zk
[centos@mesos-master1 mesos]$ cat zk
zk://10.0.1.42:2181,10.0.1.203:2181,10.0.2.123:2181/mesos
[centos@mesos-master1 mesos]$
```

As you can see, the total CPUs is 3, but allocation has been done as per the DRF. Then, it shows that the Idle is 2.5 CPUs, 1.3 GB RAM, and 11.8 GB disk. This is how it schedules and allocates the resources.

Let's quickly start one more resource, that is, an application. Now we have active tasks, which is nginx, which we just started.

Let's run one more application, that is, **Create Application**, nginx1. We will give this application 1 CPU and 400 MB of disk space. This is our long-running application.

It has been sent to **slave3**.

Now, there is one more task running, which is ngnix1, and `mesos-slave1`, and it went to **slave3**. You can see the total CPU resources are 3 CPUs, with 1.5 allocated and 1.5 idle:

```
[centos@mesos-master2 ~]$ cd /etc/mes
-bash: cd: /etc/mes: No such file or directory
[centos@mesos-master2 ~]$ cd /etc/mesos
[centos@mesos-master2 mesos]$ vi zk
[centos@mesos-master2 mesos]$ sudo vi zk
```

One thing to check here is that, earlier, 0.5 CPU was allocated to **slave2**, and now 1 CPU has been allocated to **slave3**. This happened because **slave2** only has 0.5 CPU remaining. As per resource scheduling, it was allocated to **slave3**. This is how the Mesos cluster gets resource information from all the slave servers, and allocates the resources to your required framework.

Modifying Mesos slave resources and attributes

Mesos has two basic methods to describe the agents that comprise the cluster. One of these is resources, which are managed by the Mesos master, and the other is attributes, which are simply passed onward to the frameworks using the cluster.

The resources are CPUs, memory, and disk space. For attributes, we can define whether we want a specific job to be done on a specific server, for example, if we wanted CentOS 7 to run a specific job, and, in the meantime, CentOS 5 should run any other job. We can define this in attributes. Accordingly, you can define it in the Marathon framework, or any other framework from where you want to run the job. Let's move on and look more closely at resources:

- Mesos can manage three different types of resources: scalars, ranges, and sets. These are used to represent the different resources that a Mesos slave has to offer. For example, the scalar resource type could be used to represent the amount of memory or CPU on an agent:

    - Scalar: The resource CPUs with the value 8; the resource memory with value `16384`
    - Range: The resource ports with values 1000, through 20000
    - Set: The resource disks with the values `ssd1`, `ssd2`, and `ssd3`

This is an example of the three different types of resources Mesos supports.

The disk and memory resources are specified in megabytes.

The master's user interface will convert the resource value into a more human-readable format. So, here, we can see that it's defined 16,384 resources, which will be converted to GB or MB. For example, the value 15,000 will be displayed as 14.65 GB in your Mesos cluster. By default, Mesos will try to auto-detect the resources available on the local machine when the Mesos agent starts up. So, as soon as our method agent starts up, it will auto-detect the resources and make them available to our Mesos cluster. Alternatively, we can explicitly configure which resources an agent should make available. This is where resources and attributes come in. We can make resources available by giving the following attribute:

This is how you inform the Mesos slave agent that these are the resources we need to make available. Let's look at how this works.

How to do it...

To create resources, we need to place the file in /etc/mesos-slave/resources.

The following command will create the directory, which is where you can put information in the file regarding the allocation of CPUs, memory, disk, and ports:

How it works...

At startup, the Mesos agent performs checks and sets resources to default values that are detected by the system. These resources are then overridden with the value provided by the users.

Let's look at a quick demo of how you can define resources in your Mesos slave. This is our Mesos cluster:

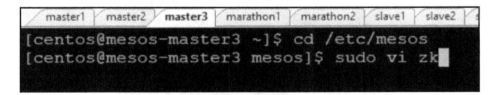

Currently, the leader is mesos-master3. If we look into agents, we can see that there is no agent registered as of now, so all the Mesos slave agents are in a stopped state. Let's check the resources. Here, the resources are 0, because there are no agents registered providing info to the Mesos cluster. Let's quickly start all three Mesos slave agents and look at how resources are allocated.

Use the following command to start the agents:

```
sudo service mesos-slave start
```

Go to Agents and you should see that `mesos-slave1` has been registered:

You can see that there are no GPUs, the memory is set to 495 MB, and the allocated disk space is 4 GB. Let's go to the Mesos homepage. Let's look at our resources. From the beginning, we started gathering all of the resources' details in our Mesos cluster. Let's start the other two slave agents as well. The resources should go up to 3 CPUs, memory should go up to 1.5 GB, and disk space should go up to 12 GB:

We have started the services. If you take a look at the status, you can see that it's in a running state. So, let's quickly move into our Mesos console and check the resource allocation table. We can see that our resources increased as soon as we started our other two slave agents. So, as I said, we have 3 CPUs, 1.5 GB memory, and 12 GB disk. If you check the agents, you will see the same thing there as well. Currently, it has exposed all the resources it has, so what we will do here is, from **slave1**, we will expose only 0.6 CPU, from **slave2**, we will expose 0.8 CPU, and from **slave3**, we will expose 0.4 CPU. In the same way, we will expose a limited amount of memory and disk from the slave servers. By doing this, we will learn how you will make use of the resources in our slave agent, and how we can define the resources to make available to the Mesos cluster according to your need. Let's go to our server and make the changes. Go into the /etc/mesos-slave directory. You need to create the resources file using the following command:

```
sudo touch resources
sudo vi resources
```

Insert the following data in the file:

```
Cpus:0.4;mem:300;disk:1024
```

Here we will make only 4 out of 10.4 CPU on **slave1** available and save it. We'll do the same thing in **slave2**—go to the mesos folder and perform touch. Edit the resource file and save it. Add the following command:

```
Cpus:0.6;mem:300;disk:1024
```

Here, we are making 6 out of 10.4 CPU available. Do the same thing on mesos-slave3, but instead of 6 we are making 0.8 out of 1 CPU available. We can see the memory we have to make available, The MB and disk is 1 GB. Save the file. Now, we will restart the Mesos slave services. Let's quickly check the status. We can see that it's activating, which takes some time.

Let's wait and see if our Mesos slave service is running. We can see it's still not coming to running state, so there might be some issue. Let's quickly check the logs-to do this, go to /var/log/mesos and use the ls command.

This is one of the troubleshooting steps. We need to check the Mesos slave error log and see what it says. If recovery failed due to a change in the configuration, and you want to keep the current agent ID, we might want to change the --reconfiguration_policy flag to a more permissive value, or what we can do is restart this agent with a new agent ID instead, and then run the following command:

```
sudo rm -f /var/lib/mesos/meta/slaves/latest
```

This will delete all the existing information and will start the slave with the latest configuration, as specified by use. If we are using the Docker containerizer, then we need to remove all the images, and then finally restart the agent. Let's go ahead and do this. We will remove the latest folder and check Docker using the following command:

```
sudo docker images
```

We can't see any images. Checking the process, we can observe that there is no process. Now, we are good to restart the Mesos slave. Check the status after restarting:

```
master1  master2  master3  marathon1  marathon2  slave1  slave2  slave3
[centos@mesos-master3 ~]$ cd /etc/mesos
[centos@mesos-master3 mesos]$ sudo vi zk
[centos@mesos-master3 mesos]$ cat zk
zk://10.0.1.42:2181,10.0.1.203:2181,10.0.2.123:2181/mesos
[centos@mesos-master3 mesos]$ 
```

We can see that it's in a running state. Now, it's a good idea to go and check the Mesos cluster. So, what we are expecting to see here is the resource that we made available on this node. Now if we check the resources file, we will see that we have exposed 0.4 CPUs, 300 MB of memory, and disk space of 1,024 MB.

Let's check the Mesos cluster UI. Here, you can see `mesos-slave1`—previously, it was only given 1 CPU, but now it has only exposed 0.4. This has happened because, when we define the resources, it takes the configuration, and only allocates according to what we defined in the resource file:

```
[centos@mesos-master1 mesos]$ cd /var/lib/zookeeper/
[centos@mesos-master1 zookeeper]$ ls -rlt
total 0
drwxr-xr-x. 2 root root 32 Mar  1 04:03 version-2
[centos@mesos-master1 zookeeper]$
```

For memory, it has allocated 300 MB, 1 GB or disk space, and it was registered a minute ago. Let's quickly restart the other two Mesos slave services.

In the other `mesos-slave` services, we need to do the same thing there as well: we need to remove the latest folder. Then, it will pick up the new configuration that we specified in the resources file. Check the Docker images. If any exist, you need to remove them. Check if any processes are running, and then restart `mesos-slave`. Check the status—here, it's in a running state. Let's quickly move to the Mesos cluster console and validate our configuration. Here, we can see the resources available, and all the Mesos slave agents as per our definition in the resources file:

```
[centos@mesos-master1 zookeeper]$ sudo touch myid
```

Let's have a look at the Mesos homepage:

```
[centos@mesos-master1 zookeeper]$ sudo vi myid
```

Normally, if we have not defined any resources, it should have taken 3 CPUs here, plus 1.5 MB memory, and 12 GB of disk space. However, due to our definition in the resources file, the total CPU allocation is 1.8, 900 MB of memory, and 3 GB of disk space is available to us.

So, this is how you can make resources available on a specific node according to your requirements. Now, let's go ahead and learn about the attributes; specifically, how you're going to define attributes, and how you will run your job according to attributes by using constraints in Marathon.

Let's examine attributes, and then we will have a quick demo on how to define attributes in your Mesos slave nodes. Attributes are used to describe certain additional information regarding the slave node, such as its OS version, whether it has a particular type of hardware, and so on. They are expressed as key value pairs, with support for three different value types: scalar, range, and text.

For example, we see how to define in a file attribute, then you can define the rack:abc xyz, then zone, east-west, you want OS CentOS 5, CentOS 6, level 10, or keys.

So, we will take the example of OS CentOS 5, 7, and 8. We will define these attributes in our slave nodes, and we will see how we will run our nginx server on different servers according to our need of using our Marathon framework.

How to do it...

To create an attribute, we need to place the file in /etc/mesos-slave/attributes.

The following command will create this directory:

```
mkdir -p, and /etc/mesos-slave/attributes
```

The filename will be the attribute label and the content will be a value. To create the os:centos attribute, simply create a file with the following contents. We are going to create an attributes file with the following content: os:centos5, centos6, and centos7, respectively, on three slave agents.

Let's define the attributes by creating an attributes file inside /etc/mesos-slave. We already have the resources with us, so now, we will create our attributes file using the following command:

```
sudo vi attributes
```

In this file, we will define slave1 as centos5. We will do the same thing in slave2, as centos6, and on slave3, as centos7. As we have changed the configuration, now we need to remove the metadata of the slave like we did last time by removing the latest folder, and we need to restart the Mesos slave services so that it will pick up the new configuration. To do this, use the following command:

```
sudo rm -f /var/lib/mesos/meta/slaves/latest
sudo service mesos-slave restart
```

Check the status. It should be in a running state. You can its status by using the following command:

```
ps -ef |grep mesos
```

This will give us our configuration. The attributes are defined here. Let's do the same thing for slave2, as follows:

```
sudo rm -f /var/lib/mesos/meta/slaves/latest
sudo service mesos-slave restart
```

Now, let's move on to slave3. Check the status—we are good here. Next, check the process. We can see that there are lots of processes running here, so let's use the following code:

```
ps-ef | grep mesos-slave
```

Now, let's move to the Marathon console and try to deploy a container.

Through Marathon, we are going to deploy an nginx server on CentOS 5, CentOS 6, and CentOS 7.

This can be done by clicking on Create Application. Enter the following details into nginx: CPUs is 0.2. We need to make sure that slave1 is only exposing 0.4 CPU, so bear that in mind.

For disk space, we will set 100 MB. For instance, simply set it to 1 in nginx. We will make the network as bridged network, the port as 80, and the name we will say nginx. After this, go to the optional section, where we will see the constraints. Here, if we remember, we have defined the attributes os:centos5, 6, and 7 to slave1, 2, and 3. We are going to define constraints here as os:, and the operator we'll use is CLUSTER, then :centos5, as shown in the following screenshot:

```
[centos@mesos-master3 zookeeper]$ cd /etc/zookeeper/conf
[centos@mesos-master3 conf]$ clear
```

By defining this, it will make sure this application gets deployed on your node, which has the attributes of centos5. Click on the **Create Application** button now. This show that it is in a running state, so say nginx and we will see it has deployed in mesos-slave1. So, our slave1 is centos5, now click on **Scale Application** and make it 2. Again, you will see that it has deployed on slave1. Now, it will not go to slave2 and slave3 because the attributes for these instances are different there:

```
[centos@mesos-master2 zookeeper]$ cd /etc/zookeeper/conf/
[centos@mesos-master2 conf]$ sudo vi zoo.cfg
```

So, let's do one thing now. We know our **slave1** is only exposing 0.4 CPU. That means that its quota has been completed now; it doesn't have any more CPU. Let's try to scale once more and see what happens. In this scenario, your two instances are deployed, but the third instance is not getting resources, so it's in a waiting state. So, let's navigate to our Mesos cluster, that is, our console, and see what happens here. In the console, we can see that the allocated CPU is 0.4, with 1.4 as Idle. This means that **slave1** resources are consumed, as we had defined only 0.4 CPU to **slave1**.

To see the allocation of our `mesos-slave1`, go to agents and you will see that the available CPU was 0.4 and that the allocated CPU now is 0.4.

Now, let's quickly run some of the applications on `mesos-slave2` and **slave3**. This application will be waiting for the resources to be allocated, but it will not get them because the **slave1** node is already full and is in a waiting state. Now, let's scale this to 2 by clicking on Scale Application. This will give you a warning to stop the current deployment. This will put the application in a running state.

Now, we will create an application that has nginx6 as the ID and enter the following details: 0.2 50 MB, 100 as CPU and memory. In Docker Container, again nginx, Network as Bridged, Port is 80. Again, we will go into the Optional section and we will change the Constraint to 6, which will be `os:CLUSTER:centos6`. Click on Create Application. You will see nginx6 running.

You can see that our nginx6 went to **slave2**. This is how we can schedule our application according to our requirements on the specific nodes. Let's check and scale ngnix6 to 2 or 3. Because we have 0.6 CPU available, so it will scale it to 3 on the same node. Let's run the application on your `centos7` node, on **slave3**. Click on **Create Application** and enter the following details: nginx7, 0.2, 100, Disk Space 100, Image, as we know, nginx, Bridged, container port 80, Name nginx, and in Optional, go in Constraints, and enter `os:CLUSTER:centos7` operator we will use CLUSTER, as `centos7`, and click on **Create Application** button.

Once you have done this, you will see that nginx7 is on **slave3**, like we wanted. Click on **Scale Application** and change it to 4; we will not be able to scale the application to more than 4 because it only has 0.8 CPU available. You will notice that it has only scaled to 3. That means, let's see how much CPU was available on **slave3**. As you can see, our memory is full, which is why our application was not able to use the remaining two CPU.

Let's change the memory and check this. To change the memory, go to the **Configuration** tab and click on Edit Application. Change the memory to 50 MB, and then click **Change and deploy configuration**, as shown in the following screenshot:

```
master1   master2   master3   marathon1   marathon2   slave1   slave2   slave3

#       http://www.apache.org/licenses/LICENSE-2.0
#
# Unless required by applicable law or agreed to in writing, software
# distributed under the License is distributed on an "AS IS" BASIS,
# WITHOUT WARRANTIES OR CONDITIONS OF ANY KIND, either express or implied.
# See the License for the specific language governing permissions and
# limitations under the License.

maxClientCnxns=50
# The number of milliseconds of each tick
tickTime=2000
# The number of ticks that the initial
# synchronization phase can take
initLimit=10
# The number of ticks that can pass between
# sending a request and getting an acknowledgement
syncLimit=5
# the directory where the snapshot is stored.
dataDir=/var/lib/zookeeper
# the port at which the clients will connect
clientPort=2181
-- INSERT -- W10: Warning: Changing a readonly file
```

Repeat this one more time. You will see that the application is in a waiting state. To avoid this, we will destroy this application and create a new application. Click on Create Application and enter the following details; Id:nginx7, CPU:0.2, Memory is 50, Disk Space 100. Here, we will need 4 Instances. Under Docker, name it nginx. Now, go to optional, enter os:CLUSTER:centos7, and click on **Create Application**. We can see it has ran all four containers on **slave3**.

In the previous section, we learned how to define resources and attributes in the Mesos slave to make the required resources available for the Mesos cluster.

Now we will look at the following concepts:

- High availability
- Fault tolerance
- Handling failures

High availability

High availability, in simple terms, means achieving very close to 100 percent system uptime by ensuring that there is no single point of failure. This is typically done by incorporating redundancy mechanisms, such as backup processes; taking our instances from the failed ones; and so on. So, by design, Mesos provides a fault-tolerant environment for running applications. The master daemon and the slave daemon operate in a distributed and highly available manner, ensuring that no one component can cause an outage of the entire cluster.

Let's learn about high availability. To ensure that Mesos is highly available to the application that uses its cluster manager, the Mesos master uses a single leader and multiple standby masters, which are ready to take over in the event that the leader's master fails. The master uses a ZooKeeper to coordinate leadership among the multiple nodes, and Mesos slaves and frameworks query ZooKeeper to determine the leading master. Let's take a look the following screenshot:

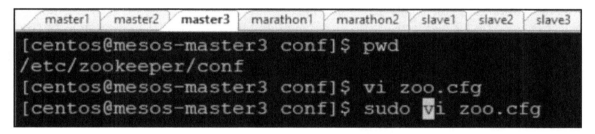

Here, the Mesos that's running is in high availability mode. We can see the frameworks. In our case, it's our Marathon. Then, we have three ZooKeepers, which have elected a leading master. The other two are in standby, and all of the others are slaves that communicate with ZooKeeper to understand who their master is. This is how Mesos runs in high availability mode if your leading master is down. Mesos master failure recovery uses a standby master. So, as soon as our leading master is down, ZooKeeper once again re-elects a new leader. In the preceding diagram, you can see that it has elected another master as a leading master, then the framework connects to the leading master, and the slave communicates with the ZooKeeper to understand who the leading master is now. This is how Mesos provides high availability to the application.

Let's quickly and practically observe exactly how this happens as soon as one of your masters goes down. We have the Mesos console; our leading master is `master3`; our other masters, `master1` and `master2`, are in standby mode. What we are going to do is stop `master3` and see what happens. You can do this using the following command:

```
sudo service mesos-master stop
```

Check the status. We can see that our Mesos master has stopped on the `master3` server. Let's quickly go to the console. The previous master was `mesos-master3`, but now the master is `mesos-master2`. Now, we've seen how high availability works for your Mesos cluster. Next, let's go ahead and understand fault tolerance and how it handles failures.

Fault tolerance

To gracefully handle failures, Mesos implements two features, both enabled by default, known as **check pointing** and **slave recovery**. Check pointing is a feature enabled in both the framework and on the slave, which allows certain information about the state of the cluster to be persistent periodically to the disk. The state of the cluster is written to the disk on the Mesos slave server. The check-pointed data includes information on the task, such as executors and status updates. The second one is slave recovery. Slave recovery allows the Mesos slave daemon to read the state from the disk, and reconnect to running executors and tasks should the Mesos slave daemon fail or be restarted. If the Mesos slave daemon fails or is restarted, slave recovery helps to read the state from the disk and reconnect to the running executors and tasks.

So, by just refreshing the Mesos cluster, we can see that both `master2` and `master1` are available for us, and that `master3` is down. `mesos-master2` is the leader. During the *Resources and Attributes* section, we ran nginx instances. `mesos-slave1` has two nginx instances, `mesos-slave3` has four, and `mesos-slave2` has three. We will stop one of the Mesos slaves and see what happens. Let's navigate to Marathon on `slave1`. For now, we can see that the URL is accessible:

```
server.1=10.0.1.42:2888:3888
server.2=10.0.1.203:2888:3888
server.3=10.0.2.123:2888:3888
```

This is the landing page for our nginx server. So, what we are going to do here is stop the Mesos slave and see if we are still able to access the landing page for both instances. Go to `slave1` and run the following command:

```
sudo service mesos-slave
```

Then stop status, and it will be stopped. Let's move to our console. We can see that `mesos-slave1` has two nginx servers running. Refresh this. Let's check the agents as well. We can still see the agent. In a few minutes, the agent will be gone, because as soon as the clusters find out that the slave is away, cluster will move the slave agent, and the resource count will also go down. Now, when we click on **Agents**, we will see only `meso-slave2` and `slave3`. Check the resources; we will see only 1 for CPU, whereas previously it was 1.8 CPU, and that the task is Running. It will not show the nginx instance, which is running on the `meso-slave1` server.

So, let's quickly refresh and see if our application is up and running. If the slave is down, we can still access our application. So, let's quickly restart the slave now. After this, with the slave running again, go to your console, refresh it, and we will see that our nginx task is back. As soon as we restarted our Mesos slave, it got the information of Task Name and again made the resources available. The CPU allocation rises to 1.8. This is how fault tolerance works for the Mesos slave, with the help of checkpointing and slave recovery. Let's quickly look at how Mesos handles failures. A number of events typically cause downtime and outages for infrastructure, including network partitions, machine failures, power outages, and so on. We will explore fault tolerance and high availability in Mesos within the context of three potential failure scenarios. The first one is machine failure, where the underlying physical or virtual host fails. In service process failure, the Mesos master or Mesos slave daemon fails. Third is upgrades. If we want to upgrade from one version to another, the Mesos master or Mesos slave daemon must be restarted. Fortunately, Mesos and the Mesos frameworks are capable of handling each of these failure modes.

We saw, with the example of the Mesos master, how high availability for the Mesos cluster can be achieved using ZooKeeper. Now, we will see what happens to the task if the Mesos slave server goes down.

So, let's quickly do an exercise on the Mesos slave. If our Mesos slave goes down, how will the task run? Let's learn how Mesos handles these failures. Currently, we have one nginx instance running, which is on `slave3`, so let's stop this `mesos-slave3` process. To do this, go into the slave 3 server and enter the following command:

```
sudo service mesos-slave stop
```

Check the status to make sure that we have stopped the service. Quickly go back to the console. As we already know, once you stop the slave process, our instance will keep on running. This is our slave service, which is on `slave3`. It'll just take some time to reload, so hang on a little while. Soon, you will see `slave3` disappear, but our process will still be running. Here, we can see that the process has gone to `mesos-slave2`.

As we saw, we have stopped `mesos-slave3`-automatically; this was detected and the service went to another server. Let's quickly check that it's still working. Let's stop the `mesos-slave2` as well now. After this, we can go to our console and check this. This confirms that one more instance was started on `slave1`. This shows that as soon as we stop one of the slaves, cluster moves the all of the tasks to another server.

Here, we learned how to install Mesos and its supporting tools and how to install the Mesos master and slaves. We also installed Marathon and Docker.

Configuration setup of Mesosphere

In this section, we will work on the configuration of our resources. In the following manner, we will configure ZooKeeper connection information for Mesos, and then we will work on the ZooKeeper configuration setup on our master servers.

We completed the installation part of our project in the previous section. During the ZooKeeper configuration setup, we will define a unique ID on all the master servers and then do a mapping of ZooKeeper IDs to actual hosts before restarting ZooKeeper. Then, we will perform Mesos configurations on the master server: we will set up a quorum, then we will configure our hostname and IP address, and then we will see how to start and stop the Mesos master. Then, we will have a look at how to configure Marathon services. We will first install Java, then we will set up ZooKeeper's configuration to connect to our Mesos cluster and then set up our configuration to store Marathon information in ZooKeeper. Then, we will see how to start and stop Marathon services, and we will allow communication between subnets in AWS.

As you know, we have already created two subnets in AWS, and there are different hosts that are divided between those subnets. We want these two subnets to communicate with each other, so we will create some rules so that our server instances can communicate from one subnet to another. Then, we will allow inbound access to the Mesos and Marathon consoles in AWS. Then, once our configuration is done, we will access the Mesos UI and Marathon. For that, we need to allow access in AWS, after which we will test high availability for our Mesos and Marathon services.

We will see how cluster setup is done, and then we will stop one server and see how Mesos responds, and how the leader election takes place after the leader is down. Next, we will see how Marathon services work. As we have two Marathon services, we will stop one and see how to deploy the services on Mesos using the other Marathon.

We will test higher availability for Mesos and Marathon services by stopping one of them, and seeing if the Marathon services are still accessible. Then, we will start Mesos slaves and register those slaves in the Mesos cluster.

Configuring ZooKeeper connection information for Mesos

Our initial step is to create ZooKeeper connection information for Mesos. This configuration enables all of our servers to connect to the correct master server. The ZooKeeper cluster will only consist of our master server's information. The master server will be only the member of our ZooKeeper cluster, and all of the servers will communicate with our master using the following configuration file. Let's see that configuration file:

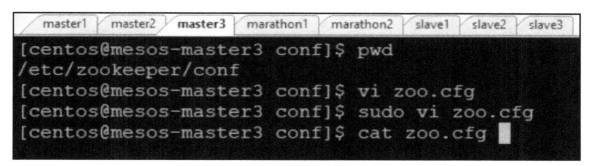

This is the ZooKeeper configuration file.

We need to complete this step by editing the file and adding the information of our three master servers. As you can see, the lines will start with zk and end with /mesos, and in-between, you'll need to paste your master server's IP addresses and ZooKeeper ports.

We will now add the master server's IP to this file:

```
server.1=10.0.1.42:2888:3888
server.2=10.0.1.203:2888:3888
server.3=10.0.2.123:2888:3888
[centos@mesos-master3 conf]$ pwd
/etc/zookeeper/conf
[centos@mesos-master3 conf]$
```

We will get the following output:

```
master1   master2   master3   marathon1   marathon2   slave1   slave2   slave3

[centos@mesos-master1 mesos]$ cat zk
zk://localhost:2181/mesos
[centos@mesos-master1 mesos]$ sudo vi zk
[centos@mesos-master1 mesos]$ cat zk
zk://10.0.1.42:2181,10.0.1.203:2181,10.0.2.123:2181/mesos
[centos@mesos-master1 mesos]$ cd /var/lib/zookeeper/
[centos@mesos-master1 zookeeper]$ ls -rlt
total 0
drwxr-xr-x. 2 root root 32 Mar  1 04:03 version-2
[centos@mesos-master1 zookeeper]$ touch myid
touch: cannot touch 'myid': Permission denied
[centos@mesos-master1 zookeeper]$ sudo touch myid
[centos@mesos-master1 zookeeper]$ vi myid
[centos@mesos-master1 zookeeper]$ sudo vi myid
[centos@mesos-master1 zookeeper]$ cd /etc/zookeeper/conf/
[centos@mesos-master1 conf]$ vi zoo.cfg
[centos@mesos-master1 conf]$ sudo vi zoo.cfg
```

Remove the local information, as shown here:

```
[centos@mesos-master2 zookeeper]$ cd /etc/zookeeper/conf/
[centos@mesos-master2 conf]$ sudo vi zoo.cfg
```

As you can see, it has given us a warning; Warning: Changing read only file. Just exit this by entering the :q command.

Let's work on adding the master server's IP address to this file:

```
sudo vi zk
```

We will get the following output:

```
# the directory where the snapshot is stored.
dataDir=/var/lib/zookeeper
# the port at which the clients will connect
clientPort=2181
server.1=10.0.1.42:2888:3888
server.2=10.0.1.203:2888:3888
server.3=10.0.2.123:2888:3888
```

Let's change the IP address, as shown here:

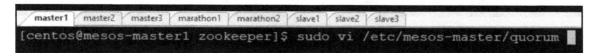

```
master1  master2  master3  marathon1  marathon2  slave1  slave2  slave3
[centos@mesos-master1 zookeeper]$ sudo vi /etc/mesos-master/quorum
```

`10.0.1.203:2181` is our second master server, and `10.0.2.123:2181` is the third one.

`10.0.2.123:2181` is from another availability zone, so our third master server is in another availability zone. Let's save the file. Now, use the `cat` command to read the file, as shown in the following screenshot:

```
[centos@mesos-master1 mesos-master]$ ls -rlt
total 8
-rw-rw-r--. 1 root root 15 Feb  8 16:22 work_dir
-rw-rw-r--. 1 root root  2 Mar  1 04:54 quorum
[centos@mesos-master1 mesos-master]$
```

Copy the marked area, because we need to add this identical entry to each of our master and slave servers. This will help each individual server to connect to the correct master server in order to communicate with the cluster.

Here, we need to enter the following commands:

```
[centos@mesos-master1 mesos-master]$ sudo touch ip
```

We get the following output:

```
[centos@mesos-master1 mesos-master]$ sudo vi ip
```

Next, paste in the line of IP addresses that we copied:

```
-- INSERT -- W10: Warning: Changing a readonly file
```

Repeat the same steps for master3. Delete zk 1L, 26C, then insert and paste in our line of IPs:

```
[centos@mesos-master1 mesos-master]$ sudo cp ip hostname
```

Here, we make sure our entries are identical on all the master and slave servers, otherwise it will impact the servers communicating with the master server.

Do the same with the slave3 server, which is our last server.

Let's quickly verify whether all three servers are here with the following command:

```
[centos@mesos-master1 mesos-master]$ ls -rlt
total 16
-rw-rw-r--. 1 root root 15 Feb  8 16:22 work_dir
-rw-rw-r--. 1 root root  2 Mar  1 04:54 quorum
-rw-r--r--. 1 root root 10 Mar  1 05:00 ip
-rw-r--r--. 1 root root 10 Mar  1 05:01 hostname
[centos@mesos-master1 mesos-master]$ clear
```

You have to make sure that the line starts with zk and ends with /mesos. In between, you have the IP address of the master server and the ZooKeeper port. We have added these identical entries in each of our master servers, so our next step is to configure the master server's ZooKeeper configuration.

On your master servers, we will need to do some additional ZooKeeper configuration. We need to define a unique ID number, starting from 1 up to 255, for each of our master servers. This information is kept inside; the path is as follows:

```
[centos@mesos-master1 mesos-master]$ cat ip
10.0.1.42
[centos@mesos-master1 mesos-master]$ cat hostname
10.0.1.42
[centos@mesos-master1 mesos-master]$ █
```

We need to make a file here with the name `myid`, as shown here:

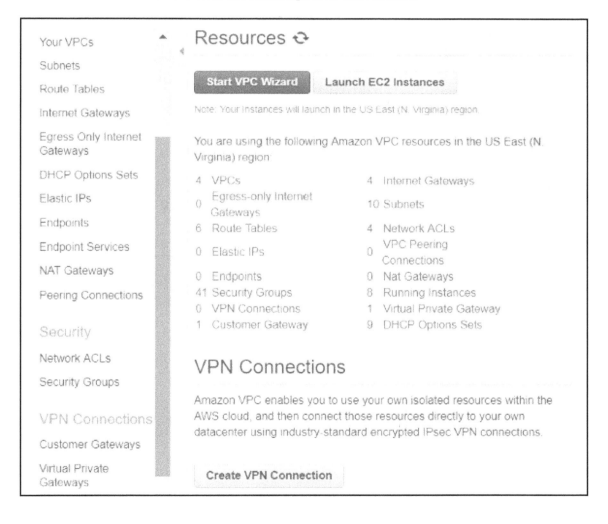

Open the file using `vi` command and enter the value as 1 since this is our first master server.

We will now move to the second master server. We will follow the same path as before, except that for our `myid` value, we will add 2 instead. This is our second master. Similarly, for our third master server, we will enter `myid` as 3.

We have now completed the second step in our setup, where we have changed the ZooKeeper configuration by adding a unique ID number for all three master servers to a file called `myid` under `var/lib/zookeeper`. Let's move to the next step.

Our next step is to change our ZooKeeper configuration file to map our ZooKeeper IDs to the actual host. This will ensure that the service can correctly resolve each host from the ID system that it uses.

Let's open the ZooKeeper configuration file:

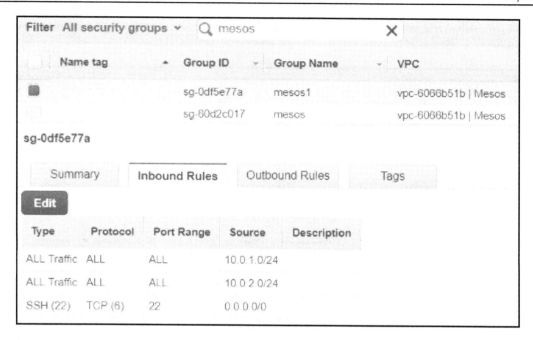

This is the path where `zoo.cfg` is stored. This is our ZooKeeper configuration file:

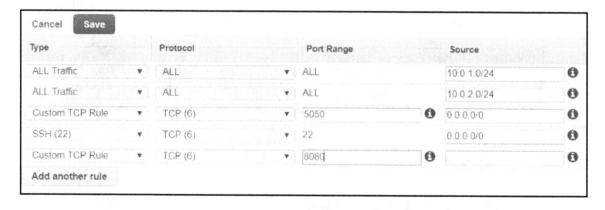

We get the following warning, Changing a read-only file. This means that we need to use sudo:

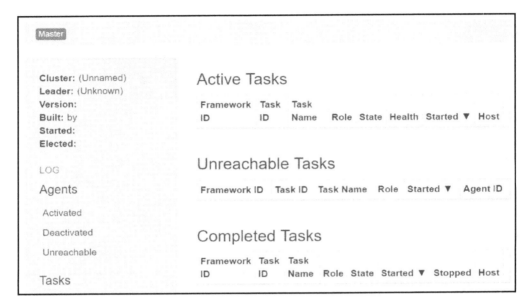

Press *Enter*, and you will get the ZooKeeper configuration file again. Go to the last line and add the following parameters:

```
master1   master2   master3
[centos@mesos-master1 ~]$ cd /etc/mesos-master/
[centos@mesos-master1 mesos-master]$ ls -rlt
```

We have server.1, which is our ID; 10.0.1.42, which is our IP address; and our port details are at the end. Similarly, we have server.2 and server.3. Now, let's save the file and run cat:

```
total 16
-rw-rw-r--. 1 root root 15 Feb  8 16:22 work_dir
-rw-rw-r--. 1 root root  2 Mar  1 04:54 quorum
drwxr-xr-x. 2 root root 45 Mar  3 06:28 bak
-rw-r--r--. 1 root root 10 Mar  3 06:49 ip
-rw-r--r--. 1 root root 10 Mar  9 14:01 hostname
```

Here, within this file, we mapped each ID to a host. The host specification includes two ports; the first for communicating with the leader, and the second for handling election when a new leader is required.

The ZooKeeper servers are identified by server, followed by dot and their ID number (for example, `server.1`). For this guide, we will be using the default port for each function, while our IDs are 1, 2, and 3. This is what our file looks like now:

```
[centos@mesos-master1 mesos-master]$ cat    hostname
10.0.1.42
[centos@mesos-master1 mesos-master]$ ▊
```

We will add the same mappings in each of our master servers' configuration files. Let's copy this and go to the `master1` server:

```
[centos@mesos-master1 mesos-master]$ hostname
```

Go to the end and insert the identical instances of all of our master servers in the ZooKeeper configuration.

Go to `master2`, as shown here:

```
[centos@mesos-master1 mesos-master]$ sudo vi hostname ▊
```

Go to the end with *Shift + G*, and add the entry, as shown here:

```
127.0.0.1    localhost localhost.localdomain localhost4 localhost4.local
domain4
::1          localhost localhost.localdomain localhost6 localhost6.local
domain6
10.0.1.42        mesos-master1
10.0.1.203       mesos-master2
10.0.2.68    mesos-master3

[centos@mesos-master1 ~]$ ▊
```

We have now added `server1`, `server2`, and `server3`. With this, our ZooKeeper configuration is completed.

Configuring Mesos on the master server

We will start by changing the quorum settings. The quorum settings should reflect your cluster size.

We need to change quorum to make decisions while electing a leader. This setting will stipulate the number of servers necessary for a cluster to be in a functioning state. The quorum setting should be so that 50 percent of master members must be present to make decisions.

We have three master servers, so the only setting that satisfies the quorum parameter is 2. We will now open the configuration file. Go to the `master1` server. Clear the screen and enter the following:

```
[centos@mesos-master2 mesos-master]$ cat /etc/hosts
127.0.0.1    localhost localhost.localdomain localhost4 localhost4.local
domain4
::1          localhost localhost.localdomain localhost6 localhost6.local
domain6
10.0.1.42        mesos-master1
10.0.1.203       mesos-master2
10.0.2.68        mesos-master3
[centos@mesos-master2 mesos-master]$
```

Change the value 1 to 2. Value 1 was the default setting. After you've updated the value, save and close the file. Repeat this on each of our remaining master servers.

Configuring the hostname and IP address

In this step, we will provide the hostname and IP address for each of our master servers. We will be using the IP address for the hostname so that our instance will not have any trouble resolving. Since you have defined the details in the hostname, you should be good, but we will not use hostname, we use the IP address only.

For our master servers, the IP address needs to be placed in this file:

```
cd /etc/mesos-master/
```

We will get the following output:

```
Redirecting to /bin/systemctl start zookeeper.service
```

We need to create a file with the name IP and hostname. Let's create a file with IP:

```
sudo touch ip
sudo vi ip,
```

We need to provide the following:

```
10.0.1.42
```

Save the file. Now, we need to create a filename with the hostname, except we will use the IP address. For this, copy the `ip` file create and name it as hostname by using the following command:

```
sudo cp ip hostname
```

Run `ls -rlt` command and you will find that both files are present:

```
    Loaded: loaded (/usr/lib/systemd/system/zookeeper.service; enabled;
vendor preset: disabled)
    Active: active (running) since Fri 2018-03-09 14:13:29 UTC; 4s ago
 Main PID: 1829 (java)
   Memory: 31.5M
   CGroup: /system.slice/zookeeper.service
           └─1829 java -Dzookeeper.log.dir=. -Dzookeeper.root.logger...

Mar 09 14:13:32 mesos-master1 zookeeper[1829]: at java.net.AbstractP...
Mar 09 14:13:32 mesos-master1 zookeeper[1829]: at java.net.AbstractP...
Mar 09 14:13:32 mesos-master1 zookeeper[1829]: at java.net.AbstractP...
Mar 09 14:13:32 mesos-master1 zookeeper[1829]: at java.net.SocksSock...
Mar 09 14:13:32 mesos-master1 zookeeper[1829]: at java.net.Socket.co...
Mar 09 14:13:32 mesos-master1 zookeeper[1829]: at org.apache.zookeep...
Mar 09 14:13:32 mesos-master1 zookeeper[1829]: at org.apache.zookeep...
Mar 09 14:13:32 mesos-master1 zookeeper[1829]: at org.apache.zookeep...
Mar 09 14:13:32 mesos-master1 zookeeper[1829]: at org.apache.zookeep...
Mar 09 14:13:32 mesos-master1 zookeeper[1829]: 2018-03-09 14:13:32,8...
```

So, we have now created both files, as shown here:

```
94] - Processed session termination for sessionid: 0x1620ac11d970005
Mar 09 14:14:04 mesos-master2 zookeeper[2674]: 2018-03-09 14:14:04,002
[myid:2] - INFO [ProcessThread(sid:2 cport:-1)::PrepRequestProcessor@4
94] - Processed session termination for sessionid: 0x1620ac11d970002
Mar 09 14:14:04 mesos-master2 zookeeper[2674]: 2018-03-09 14:14:04,003
[myid:2] - INFO [ProcessThread(sid:2 cport:-1)::PrepRequestProcessor@4
94] - Processed session termination for sessionid: 0x3620ac05ddc0000
Mar 09 14:14:04 mesos-master2 zookeeper[2674]: 2018-03-09 14:14:04,003
[myid:2] - INFO [ProcessThread(sid:2 cport:-1)::PrepRequestProcessor@4
94] - Processed session termination for sessionid: 0x1620ac11d970003
Mar 09 14:14:04 mesos-master2 zookeeper[2674]: 2018-03-09 14:14:04,003
[myid:2] - INFO [ProcessThread(sid:2 cport:-1)::PrepRequestProcessor@4
94] - Processed session termination for sessionid: 0x1620aa7aade0001
Mar 09 14:14:04 mesos-master2 zookeeper[2674]: 2018-03-09 14:14:04,003
[myid:2] - INFO [ProcessThread(sid:2 cport:-1)::PrepRequestProcessor@4
94] - Processed session termination for sessionid: 0x3620ac6089f0000
Mar 09 14:14:04 mesos-master2 zookeeper[2674]: 2018-03-09 14:14:04,003
[myid:2] - INFO [ProcessThread(sid:2 cport:-1)::PrepRequestProcessor@4
```

Similarly, we need to do this for each of our master servers.

We have thus completed the configuration of adding the IP address and hostname for the Mesos master.

Configuring Marathon services

Now that we have completed Mesos configuration, we will start on configuring Marathon. Marathon will run on two separate hosts, `marathon1` and `marathon2`, and will be used to assign jobs to Mesos. Only the Mesos master server will be able to schedule jobs. Before we begin, let's first install Java using the following command:

```
sudo yum insall java-1.8.0-openjdk-devel
```

We are using Java 1.8. To validate the version by using `java -version` command, you can see that we have installed version 1.8.0_161. Copy the command to install Java and execute it on `marathon2` server. With that, we are done with the installation of Java.

Now, we need to define the list of ZooKeeper masters that Marathon will connect to for information and scheduling. We will be using the same ZooKeeper connection that we have been using for Mesos. To add a list of ZooKeeper master servers, go to the following directory, `/etc/systemd/system/multi-user.target.wants`, and open the `marathon.service` file.

Here, in the ExecStart section, we need to add `--master` and the details of the ZooKeeper server IP and port at the end of the line. You will find these details in our master servers, which can be read using the following command:

```
cat /etc/mesos/zk
```

Copy the configuration and add it at the end of the line ExecStart. This configuration will allow our Marathon service to connect to the Mesos cluster. We also want Marathon to store its own state information in ZooKeeper. This can be done by adding the ZooKeeper information as `--zk`. Paste the ZooKeeper IP again, and now change mesos to marathon at the end of the IP. Now, we will provide the hostname, which is our IP address. IP addresses can be found by using `ifconfig`. Hence, the final `ExecStart` will look something similar to the following screenshot:

You need to copy the information that you just wrote, as we need to put this information in our `marathon1` server. In `marathon1`, navigate to `/etc/systemd/system`, and open the file using the following command:

```
sudo vi marathon.service
```

Go to the `ExecStart` line and paste the content you copied. Now, you need to change the hostname, which is found using `ipconfig`. Paste the hostname and save the file. Once the file is closed, and you've restarted the Marathon service, it will start the Marathon service with the information we have given it on Mesos and Marathon. This setup for Marathon will be used to configure during Marathon's startup. That is, while starting up, it will look up those details and start the Marathon services with those configurations.

Now, let's start all the services and verify Marathon and Mesos using the browser. Before doing that, we need to allow communication between the subnets. We will make changes in the security group to allow inbound connections from another subnet. Travel to the EC2 Dashboard and click on Running Instances. Here, you will find the eight servers that we have created. Select the server on one subnet with the address of 10.0.1.42.

Just a reminder that we created two subnets. You can verify this by visiting the VPC Dashboard and click on **Subnets**. As you are aware, we have a server inside this subnet, and our goal is to make sure that the subnets communicate with each other on the ports, as Marathon, and on one of the master servers. We have deliberately kept one of the masters on on subnet, and all of the other servers on another subnet. Our Marathon master and slave is on one subnet, and another group of Marathon masters is on another subnet.

Here, we want these two subnets to communicate with each other, so we need to allow communication between them. To achieve this, we need to make changes in security groups. Let's go to EC2 Instances, click on Running Instances, and then click on one of the instances and check the security group. Click on the security group, and you can check the inbound tab.

Since we need to allow this traffic. Click on edit and you will find one inbound rule present that we added while creating the server, which is SSH. Before we allow communication, let's check if these subnets can communicate between themselves or not. We will be using telnet to check communication. The following command contains the IP of master3, which is on another server:

```
telnet 10.0.2.123 5050
```

You will notice that we are not able to connect to the server. Let's try using the ZooKeeper port to check; you will find that you are not able to connect to the server that way either.

Now, navigate to the EC2 Dashboard, and click on **Running Instances**. Now, select another subnet, 10.0.2.0/24, and click the security group. You can see that only SSH is allowed for now. To add more rules, click on Edit, and then Add Rule. Under the type dropdown, select All traffic, and enter the IP as 10.0.1.0/24. This is for restricting our traffic. This means that, apart from this subnet, no one can access those servers on those ports. Click on **Save** and our security group will similar.

Add another rule to allow traffic into another subnet as well. This time, add the IP as 10.0.2.0/24. Here, we are restricting access only to this subnet. Click on **Save**, and then we are done allowing traffic between the two subnets.

Let's verify what we did by using telnet 10.0.2.123 on master1 again. This time, you will see that we are able to connect to it. Check the same for the ZooKeeper port and you will notice that we are able to connect there also.

Now, you need to check whether you are able to connect to the internal subnet on `10.0.1.203`. You should find that you are not able to connect. You can see that our ports are active, but still, we are not able to connect the internet to the subnet. We are able, however, to connect another subnet to the first subnet. To allow us to connect to this, let's first add one more rule in the security group. Go to Mesos, click on **Security Group**, then click **Edit**, and add **Rule**. Here, we will select type as All traffic, and add `0.0.1.0/24` as the IP, then click on **Save**. We need to add this rule so that our instances can communicate with each other inside that security group. Now, make the same changes for the other security group. Here, we will add `10.0.2.0/24` as the IP. Quickly validate both the security groups, and we can see that we have added a rule where instances can communicate with each other from different security groups, as well as from inside the same security group. We will try to communicate between `master1` and `master2`. Quickly check this using the command telnet `10.0.1.203 2181`. Now, we are able to successfully communicate between our instances.

Let's go ahead and restart the services. First, we will stop all the services and then we will start them again, starting from mesos in `master1`. The following are the commands to stop the services:

```
sudo service mesos-master stop
sudo service mesos-slave stop
sudo service zookeeper stop
```

Now, stop all the services in `master2` and `master3`, and then stop the slave services in all slaves instances using the `sudo service mesos-slave stop` command. Once all the services are stopped, we will now start them all again.

Let's go to `master1`, and enter `sudo service mesos-master stop`. To check the status, run the `sudo service mesos-master status` command. It gives an error, stating `ZOO_ERROR@handle_socket_error: Socket`, Connection refused: server refused to accept the client. That means that it is trying to check ZooKeeper.

To avoid this error, we will stop `mesos-master` first, and then we will start ZooKeeper:

```
sudo service zookeeer start
```

Check the status and start ZooKeeper only on all the masters. Once you have started all of the ZooKeeper instances, and up on checking the status, you will find that it has started performing the negotiation.

Let's start the master server now, with the following command:

```
service mesos-master start, do sudo, say status.
```

Now, we need to start all the services that we stopped previously in all our instances. This is `master2`, `master3`, and all 3 of the slave instances. Once all of the services are on, we will now start with Marathon service by using the `sudo service marathon start` command. We are getting an error which says, marathon.service change on disk. To find out more about the error, run `systemctl daemon-reload`. We changed the path earlier, hence we need to add the path as a parameter. Now we need to run the `systemctl daemon-reload`. Again, start the services. So, we have executed this service. Use service marathon start to start the service. It will take a long time to find out why this is the case, visit `var/log/` messages with the following commands:

```
cd /var/log/
sudo vi messages
```

Here, you can see we get the same error: `java.lang.UnsatisfiedLinkError`: no mesos in `java.library.path`.

This means that we need to install Mesos here, too, by using the following command:

```
sudo yum install mesos
```

We will just use those libraries to start our Marathon. Here, we are done with installation of Mesos.

Let's start the Marathon service using the following:

```
service marathon start
```

Check the message file again to view if there are still any errors. This is done by using the following commands:

```
cd /var/log/ sudo vi messages
sudo tail -f messages
```

Now, you will see that we are not able to see any errors, which means that we have all of services up and running. This means that we have successfully started Marathon.

You will see the Marathon log in `var/log/messages`. Now, we need to perform the installation that we just did in `Marathon2`.

Let's install Apache Mesos. Mesos is already installed here, so we may not find any issue during installation here, so let's quickly start the services. Use service marathon start to see the status. We can see it's active and running. Just check the status -l to see the logs-this shows that we have got all the services up and running, so Marathon must be started now. Our next step is to browse these services. So, let's quickly grab the IP of all three masters, and see if we are able to access the services through a browser. Let's go to EC2 Instances, click **Running Instances**, and check your master IP, to find this, you need to check the Public IP.

Allowing inbound access to Mesos and Marathon console in AWS

Let's make changes in our security group to allow access to the ports of Marathon and Mesos. Let's go to the VPC Dashboard and click on **Security Groups**:

```
er@162] - Created server with tickTime 2000 minSessionTimeout 4000 maxS
essionTimeout 40000 datadir /var/lib/zookeeper/version-2 snapdir /var/l
ib/zookeeper/version-2
Mar 09 14:13:55 mesos-master3 zookeeper[2122]: 2018-03-09 14:13:55,434
[myid:3] - INFO  [QuorumPeer[myid=3]/0:0:0:0:0:0:0:2181:Follower@63]
- FOLLOWING - LEADER ELECTION TOOK - 34
Mar 09 14:13:55 mesos-master3 zookeeper[2122]: 2018-03-09 14:13:55,452
[myid:3] - INFO  [QuorumPeer[myid=3]/0:0:0:0:0:0:0:2181:Learner@323]
- Getting a diff from the leader 0x160000004d
Mar 09 14:13:55 mesos-master3 zookeeper[2122]: 2018-03-09 14:13:55,457
[myid:3] - INFO  [QuorumPeer[myid=3]/0:0:0:0:0:0:0:2181:FileTxnSnapLo
g@240] - Snapshotting: 0x160000004d to /var/lib/zookeeper/version-2/sna
pshot.160000004d
Mar 09 14:14:01 mesos-master3 zookeeper[2122]: 2018-03-09 14:14:01,168
[myid:3] - WARN  [QuorumPeer[myid=3]/0:0:0:0:0:0:0:2181:Follower@118]
- Got zxid 0x1700000001 expected 0x1
Mar 09 14:14:01 mesos-master3 zookeeper[2122]: 2018-03-09 14:14:01,168
[myid:3] - INFO  [SyncThread:3:FileTxnLog@199] - Creating new log file:
```

We can search our security group for mesos as follows:

```
master1   master2   master3
-rw-------. 1 root    root         4499 Mar  2 12:11 yum.log
-rw-r--r--. 1 root    root          483 Mar  2 19:07 1
-rw-------. 1 root    root         1424 Mar  8 17:33 maillog-20180308
-rw-------. 1 root    root     17852263 Mar  8 18:46 messages-20180308
-rw-------. 1 root    root       260800 Mar  8 18:46 secure-20180308
-rw-r--r--. 1 root    root        12491 Mar  8 18:47 cron-20180308
-rw-------. 1 root    root            0 Mar  8 18:47 spooler
-rw-r--r--. 1 root    root        31863 Mar  9 11:40 dmesg.old
-rw-r--r--. 1 root    root        31906 Mar  9 12:12 dmesg
-rw-r--r--. 1 root    root          831 Mar  9 12:12 boot.log
-rw-------. 1 root    root          412 Mar  9 12:12 maillog
-rw-------. 1 root    root       827684 Mar  9 12:12 cloud-init.log
-rw-------. 1 root    utmp        59904 Mar  9 13:54 btmp
-rw-rw-r--. 1 root    utmp        41088 Mar  9 13:58 wtmp
-rw-r--r--. 1 root    root       292292 Mar  9 13:58 lastlog
drwxrwxr-x. 2 root    root        28672 Mar  9 14:00 mesos
-rw-r--r--. 1 root    root         3022 Mar  9 14:01 cron
```

Then we need to check the Inbound Rules, as shown in the following screenshot:

zk://10.0.1.42:2181,10.0.1.203:2181,10.0.2.68:2181/mesos

You can see that currently, access has been granted to SSH on TCP Port 22 from any source. Let's click **Edit**, and then click on **Add another rule**. We will add a custom rule, with port 5050 and the Destination as anywhere. As a best practice, you should restrict the source to your IP address, but for this example, we will use any source. Save the following:

We will add another rule-the first was for Marathon, and the other is for our Apache Mesos access.

Do the same thing for another security group: **Edit**, add custom rule, 5050. Save it. Let's see if we can access it now:

```
sudo service mesos-slave start
sudo service mesos-slave stop
```

Yes, we are able to access it!

After accessing the console, we can see that the cluster and leader are unknown and unnamed. So, let's quickly see how we can resolve this issue.

Log into the console, and then log in to the three master servers and change it to the following:

```
master1  master2  master3

[centos@mesos-master1 ~]$ cd /etc/mesos-master/
[centos@mesos-master1 mesos-master]$ ls -rlt
```

This gives us the following output:

```
total 16
-rw-rw-r--. 1 root root 15 Feb  8 16:22 work_dir
-rw-rw-r--. 1 root root  2 Mar  1 04:54 quorum
drwxr-xr-x. 2 root root 45 Mar  3 06:28 bak
-rw-r--r--. 1 root root 10 Mar  3 06:49 ip
-rw-r--r--. 1 root root 10 Mar  9 14:01 hostname
```

Here, you can see the hostname:

```
[centos@mesos-master1 mesos-master]$ cat   hostname
10.0.1.42
[centos@mesos-master1 mesos-master]$
```

We get an IP:

We will change this `hostname` to our actual hostname:

```
[centos@mesos-master1 mesos-master]$ hostname
mesos-master1
```

The hostname is the following:

```
mesos-master1
```

Then, we need to insert the `hostname` in the `hostname` file:

```
[centos@mesos-master1 mesos-master]$ sudo vi hostname
```

We need to do the same changes on all the servers. First, we check the hostname, and change it to `mesos-master`. Change the hostname to `mesos-master2`. Do the same changes in `master3`. Check the hostname, since we have changed the file from IP to hostname of the server. After this, we need to make sure that our host entries are correct.

Let's quickly check whether our host entries are correct or not by executing the following command line:

```
cat /etc/hosts
```

The preceding command line generates the following output:

```
127.0.0.1    localhost localhost.localdomain localhost4 localhost4.local
domain4
::1          localhost localhost.localdomain localhost6 localhost6.local
domain6
10.0.1.42         mesos-master1
10.0.1.203        mesos-master2
10.0.2.68         mesos-master3

[centos@mesos-master1 ~]$
```

As you see here, we have already made these changes to save ourselves time. This should point to our private IP on all the three servers.

We will quickly validate by again using the earlier command line, as shown in the following screenshot:

```
master1   master2   master3
[centos@mesos-master2 mesos-master]$ cat /etc/hosts
127.0.0.1    localhost localhost.localdomain localhost4 localhost4.local
domain4
::1          localhost localhost.localdomain localhost6 localhost6.local
domain6
10.0.1.42        mesos-master1
10.0.1.203       mesos-master2
10.0.2.68        mesos-master3
[centos@mesos-master2 mesos-master]$
```

This is where you can see that I have made the host changes. We will restart the servers, starting with `master1`. First, we will start the ZooKeeper by executing the following command line:

```
sudo service zookeeper start
```

The preceding command line will generate the following output:

```
Redirecting to /bin/systemctl start zookeeper.service
```

Let's check with the status of the server by executing the following command line:

```
sudo service zookeeper status
```

You can see that the server is running:

```
   Loaded: loaded (/usr/lib/systemd/system/zookeeper.service; enabled;
vendor preset: disabled)
   Active: active (running) since Fri 2018-03-09 14:13:29 UTC; 4s ago
 Main PID: 1829 (java)
   Memory: 31.5M
   CGroup: /system.slice/zookeeper.service
           └─1829 java -Dzookeeper.log.dir=. -Dzookeeper.root.logger...

Mar 09 14:13:32 mesos-master1 zookeeper[1829]: at java.net.AbstractP...
Mar 09 14:13:32 mesos-master1 zookeeper[1829]: at java.net.AbstractP...
Mar 09 14:13:32 mesos-master1 zookeeper[1829]: at java.net.AbstractP...
Mar 09 14:13:32 mesos-master1 zookeeper[1829]: at java.net.SocksSock...
Mar 09 14:13:32 mesos-master1 zookeeper[1829]: at java.net.Socket.co...
Mar 09 14:13:32 mesos-master1 zookeeper[1829]: at org.apache.zookeep...
Mar 09 14:13:32 mesos-master1 zookeeper[1829]: at org.apache.zookeep...
Mar 09 14:13:32 mesos-master1 zookeeper[1829]: at org.apache.zookeep...
Mar 09 14:13:32 mesos-master1 zookeeper[1829]: at org.apache.zookeep...
Mar 09 14:13:32 mesos-master1 zookeeper[1829]: 2018-03-09 14:13:32,8...
```

Copy this and run it on all other servers where the ZooKeeper log shows status -1:

```
sudo service zookeeper status -1
```

You will see that it will perform all the work required to elect the leader:

```
94] - Processed session termination for sessionid: 0x1620ac11d970005
Mar 09 14:14:04 mesos-master2 zookeeper[2674]: 2018-03-09 14:14:04,002
[myid:2] - INFO  [ProcessThread(sid:2 cport:-1)::PrepRequestProcessor@4
94] - Processed session termination for sessionid: 0x1620ac11d970002
Mar 09 14:14:04 mesos-master2 zookeeper[2674]: 2018-03-09 14:14:04,003
[myid:2] - INFO  [ProcessThread(sid:2 cport:-1)::PrepRequestProcessor@4
94] - Processed session termination for sessionid: 0x3620ac05ddc0000
Mar 09 14:14:04 mesos-master2 zookeeper[2674]: 2018-03-09 14:14:04,003
[myid:2] - INFO  [ProcessThread(sid:2 cport:-1)::PrepRequestProcessor@4
94] - Processed session termination for sessionid: 0x1620ac11d970003
Mar 09 14:14:04 mesos-master2 zookeeper[2674]: 2018-03-09 14:14:04,003
[myid:2] - INFO  [ProcessThread(sid:2 cport:-1)::PrepRequestProcessor@4
94] - Processed session termination for sessionid: 0x1620aa7aade0001
Mar 09 14:14:04 mesos-master2 zookeeper[2674]: 2018-03-09 14:14:04,003
[myid:2] - INFO  [ProcessThread(sid:2 cport:-1)::PrepRequestProcessor@4
94] - Processed session termination for sessionid: 0x3620ac6089f0000
Mar 09 14:14:04 mesos-master2 zookeeper[2674]: 2018-03-09 14:14:04,003
[myid:2] - INFO  [ProcessThread(sid:2 cport:-1)::PrepRequestProcessor@4
```

You can see this log in the `var/log/messages` files, as well, which has given the
`QuorumPeer[myid]` by running the `sudo service zookeeper status` command:

```
er@162] - Created server with tickTime 2000 minSessionTimeout 4000 maxS
essionTimeout 40000 datadir /var/lib/zookeeper/version-2 snapdir /var/l
ib/zookeeper/version-2
Mar 09 14:13:55 mesos-master3 zookeeper[2122]: 2018-03-09 14:13:55,434
[myid:3] - INFO   [QuorumPeer[myid=3]/0:0:0:0:0:0:0:0:2181:Follower@63]
- FOLLOWING - LEADER ELECTION TOOK - 34
Mar 09 14:13:55 mesos-master3 zookeeper[2122]: 2018-03-09 14:13:55,452
[myid:3] - INFO   [QuorumPeer[myid=3]/0:0:0:0:0:0:0:0:2181:Learner@323]
- Getting a diff from the leader 0x160000004d
Mar 09 14:13:55 mesos-master3 zookeeper[2122]: 2018-03-09 14:13:55,457
[myid:3] - INFO   [QuorumPeer[myid=3]/0:0:0:0:0:0:0:0:2181:FileTxnSnapLo
g@240] - Snapshotting: 0x160000004d to /var/lib/zookeeper/version-2/sna
pshot.160000004d
Mar 09 14:14:01 mesos-master3 zookeeper[2122]: 2018-03-09 14:14:01,168
[myid:3] - WARN   [QuorumPeer[myid=3]/0:0:0:0:0:0:0:0:2181:Follower@118]
- Got zxid 0x1700000001 expected 0x1
Mar 09 14:14:01 mesos-master3 zookeeper[2122]: 2018-03-09 14:14:01,168
[myid:3] - INFO   [SyncThread:3:FileTxnLog@199] - Creating new log file:
```

Currently, we are running the `master3` server, which will give the ID as 3, and this will
show `LEADER ELECTION TOOK 34` seconds:

This is all the info you will be able to. You can even go to cd /var/log and perform the vi messages by executing the sudo vi messages command, and you will see the same info as what you are trying to see in status -1:

```
  master1   master2   master3

-rw-------. 1 root   root       4499 Mar  2 12:11 yum.log
-rw-r--r--. 1 root   root        483 Mar  2 19:07 1
-rw-------. 1 root   root       1424 Mar  8 17:33 maillog-20180308
-rw-------. 1 root   root   17852263 Mar  8 18:46 messages-20180308
-rw-------. 1 root   root     260800 Mar  8 18:46 secure-20180308
-rw-r--r--. 1 root   root      12491 Mar  8 18:47 cron-20180308
-rw-------. 1 root   root          0 Mar  8 18:47 spooler
-rw-r--r--. 1 root   root      31863 Mar  9 11:40 dmesg.old
-rw-r--r--. 1 root   root      31906 Mar  9 12:12 dmesg
-rw-r--r--. 1 root   root        831 Mar  9 12:12 boot.log
-rw-------. 1 root   root        412 Mar  9 12:12 maillog
-rw-------. 1 root   root     827684 Mar  9 12:12 cloud-init.log
-rw-------. 1 root   utmp      59904 Mar  9 13:54 btmp
-rw-rw-r--. 1 root   utmp      41088 Mar  9 13:58 wtmp
-rw-r--r--. 1 root   root     292292 Mar  9 13:58 lastlog
drwxrwxr-x. 2 root   root      28672 Mar  9 14:00 mesos
-rw-r--r--. 1 root   root       3022 Mar  9 14:01 cron
```

This is how you can check the logs and troubleshoot if you come across any issues while connecting to ZooKeeper, because all three servers connect to each other and together elect the leader.

Now, let's quickly start our Mesos service by executing the following command line:

```
sudo service mesos-master start
```

The preceding command line starts our Mesos service as shown in the following screenshot:

You will see the server is in a running state and now keep the status as -1 for detecting a new leader:

So, let's clear the screen and do the same stuff on all of the other servers again:

You will see that the server is in a running state.

To get more info, you can check with your ZooKeeper group PIDs. ZooKeeper is communicating with the Mesos master server to elect the leader, which is assigned status – 1. We will try to log in to our Mesos console for all three servers when = `Mesos` = is running.

Before logging in to the server, we need to make sure that our DNS host entries are available on your local server, that is, the local desktop machine from which you are going to access the Mesos console. Do this by adding the public IP with the name of our `mesos-master1`, `master2`, and `master3` servers, and save them on the local system from which you will access Mesos.

Summary

In this chapter, we have seen how Mesos handles failures and makes sure that your application is always running on one of the available servers. We have seen how Mesos handles failures, and during upgrades, how you can move all of your tasks to another server.

In this chapter, we covered the most important aspects for configuring Mesosphere. Let's quickly wrap up this chapter and see what we have learned. We learned how to configure ZooKeeper connection information for Mesos. We worked on ZoopKeeper and worked on Mesos configuration on master server. We then set up a rule to allow communication between subnets in AWS. Then, we tested higher availability for Mesos and Marathon services. We also saw how it is useful in high availability mode, as there is no downtime.

In the next chapter, you will see how to deploy services using Marathon on the Mesosphere cluster.

Deploying Services on Mesos Cluster

5

A service deployment is a process where we configure a collection of services in the host application that are required to instantiate the program. In this chapter, we will deploy WordPress and the nginx application via the Marathon framework. We will see how we can scale the application very quickly and easily. We will load balance our Marathon console using Elastic Load Balancer. We will also do the same process for our Mesos console. This will help us to save time as we don't have to log in each console every time. If your load balancer is forwarding a request to a standby server, then the standby will forward that request to our elected leader of Mesos. In this way, you will achieve the high availability and the resilience of Marathon and your Mesos master servers.

We will also see how to set a Marathon-lb HAProxy to load balance your customer request. Marathon-lb is a service discovery and load balancing tool for Marathon based on HAProxy. As soon as your new service is discovered in the cluster, Marathon-lb will detect that and make the changes in its configuration so new services can be consumed by our customers. This helps us to save the manual intuition of the administrator, and it automatically manages the high availability and resilience for your application.

Following are the main topics that you will get to learn as you progress with the chapter:

- Configure AWS Load Balancer for Marathon and Mesos master
- Enable the containerizer flag on all of our master slave servers, and add a Marathon user on our slave and master server where we want to deploy the services
- Deploy a sample nginx server on our Mesos cluster
- Scale the nginx server
- Set up an RDS MySQL database for WordPress
- Deploy a WordPress container in Mesos cluster
- Deploy Marathon-lb based on HAProxy for our WordPress container

Deploying applications to clusters

Before we start deploying the application to the cluster, we'll check what is the current status of the environment. As seen in the following diagram, we have three Mesos masters and two Marathon servers. So, Mesos master has three consoles because we are using three servers, and Marathon has two consoles because we are using two Marathon servers. We need to manage all three consoles every time we need to log in on each console to validate the application status, and the same goes with Marathon to check the information about your application and where it is deployed. Logging into each console every time is time consuming and it takes more effort, so to avoid this we will set up two load balancers in AWS: one for Mesos master, and another for Marathon console.

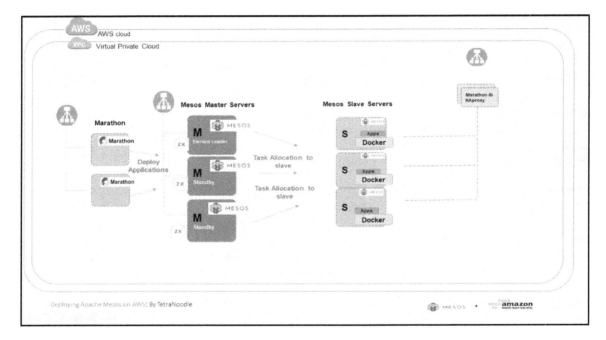

So, what is load balancing? Elastic Load Balancing automatically distributes incoming traffic across multiple targets. If any instance is down, it will not send traffic on that instance and port, and will keep sending to other instances and ports which are up and running. So, here: you get high availability and you don't have to manage each console every time. So, this is going to make our life easy.

1. Now, let's set up a load balancer by visiting the EC2 dashboard. On EC2 dashboard, go to **Load Balancers** and click on **Create Load Balancer**. Select **Application Load Balancer** and click on **Create**:

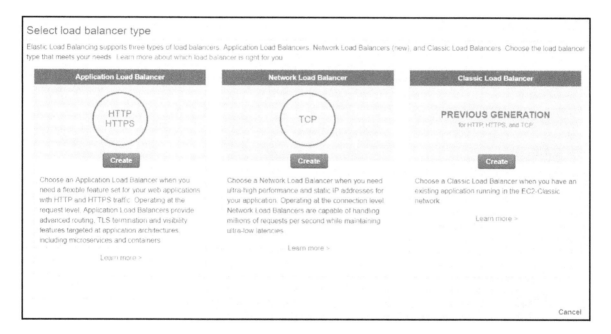

2. Now, we need to provide a name; as we are using Mesos master, we will enter `lb-mesos-master`, and then select **Scheme** as **internet-facing** load balancer, the **IP address type** as the `ipv4`, and for Listeners, **Load Balancer Protocol** would be `HTTP` and **Load Balancer Port** is `80`:

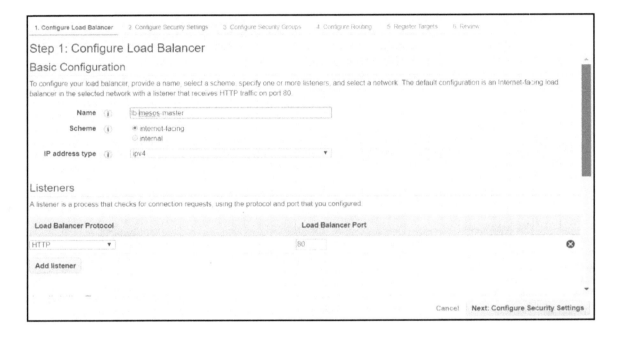

3. Now we need to add our **Availability Zones**, so we'll select **VPC** and select both the availability zones because two master servers are on one availability zone, and the third one is on another. The same will apply to Marathon—one on **east-1a** and another one **east-1b**. Then click **Next**:

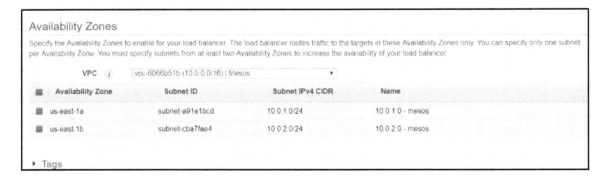

4. Next, select **Configure Security Setting**. We are using HTTP 80 port here, not HTTPS. Then click on **Next: Configure Security Groups**.

> I would recommend to use HTTPS, but it's not compulsory.

5. On **Configure Security Groups**, check the **Create a new security group** radiobox. Enter **Security group name** as lb-mesos, **Type** to Custom TCP, **Protocol** to TCP, **Port Range** to 80, and **Source** to Anywhere:

6. So, you will access this load balancer on port 80 and the source will be Anywhere. You can restrict this to your specific IP address but, as of now, we're using Anywhere. Click on **Next: Configure Routing**, enter mesos-master as **Name**, and set **Protocol** to HTTP and **Port** to 5050 because our Mesos runs on 5050. Select **Target type** to instance. The **Health checks** settings will stay on default, and then you can click on **Next: Register Targets**:

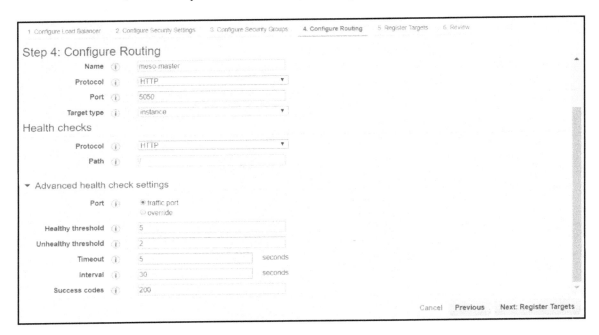

7. Now we need to select our three master servers in register targets, so click on **Add to registered** and the port should be 5050, which we have already defined. Then click **Next: Review**:

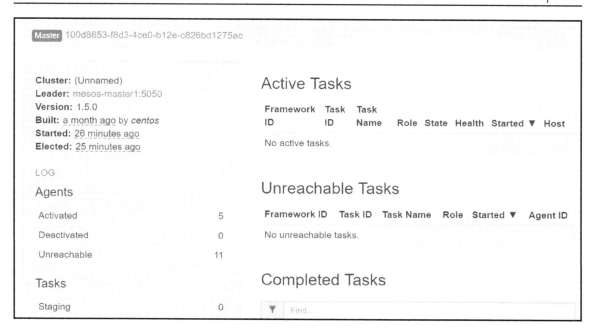

8. Now we will validate it in the **Review** step. You will see **Load balancer**, the **Security group**, the **Routing**, where we have created **New target group**, for which the name is mesos-master, and the targets. You will also see the instance IDs, which are on port 5050. Then click on **Create**. Now the creation will start. Let's look at the load balancer. The state is provisioning, so it will take some time to provision your load balancer. After some time, **State** will become active, so our load balancer is provisioned to us now. We will need the DNS name to access our application.

9. Before accessing, let's tail the logs of Mesos master. Run the `sudo tail -f /var/log/messages` command. We need to tail all three servers to see where our request goes. Now copy the DNS name and paste it in a browser:

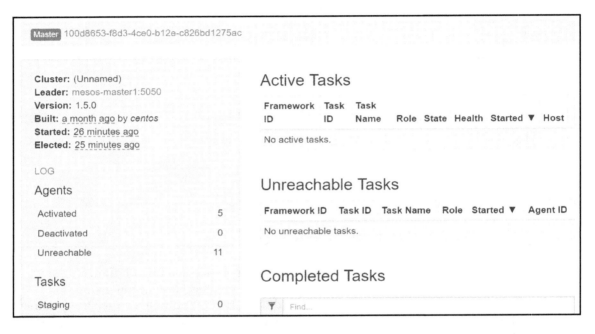

The output shows we are able to connect.

10. Now we'll see on which master it is running. Only the `master1` log is moving—that means it has connected to `master1`. Let's stop this `master1` and see what happens. So, currently our leader is `mesos-master1`: press *Ctrl + C* and run `sudo service mesos-master stop`. So, we have stopped the `master1` master. After refreshing, it will see the instance is down and it will forward our request to another available Mesos master:

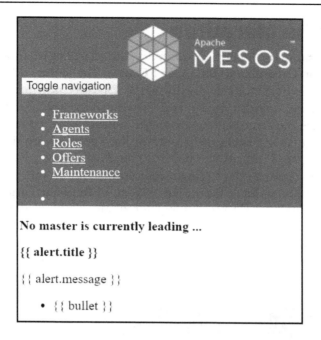

It will take time, depending on how you have set your monitoring in AWS. If you have set more time, then it will take some time. After some time, we will see our console is up and running again. As we have stopped `master1`, the request will go to `master2` and, in `master3`, we can see the normal logs updating. Load balancer is very helpful for managing our Mesos master console. The same we will set up for `marathon1` and `marathon2` as well. You can see our cluster has changed, so now the leading is Mesos master: `mesos-master2` has control and it will take care of the rest of the stuff. Now start our `master1` master back by running the `sudo service mesos-master start` command.

Setting up the Marathon

Now, let's set up the same for Marathon. Go to the EC2 dashboard and create the load balancer by clicking on **Create Load Balancer | Create**. The name will be lb-marathon; otherwise, everything remains the same. On the **Configure Security Groups** page, select **Create a new security group**, and the security group name will be lb-marathon. We will use the same 80 port from **Anywhere**. Next, on the **Configure Routing** page, we need to select **New target group** and, for the **Target group** field, the name will be marathon-targetgroup, **Protocol** will be HTTP, the **Port** will be 8080, and **Target type** is instance. You can manipulate the setting as per your requirement. So, it will quickly detect the unhealthy node and it will remove it. Next, in **Register Targets**, we'll select two Marathon servers, then we will add to the registered. Now review all the settings and click on **Create**. On the dashboard, we will see its state as provisioning and then as active. So, now our Marathon load balancer is up and running. Copy the DNS name and paste it in the browser so it will access one of the Marathon servers and provide the following results:

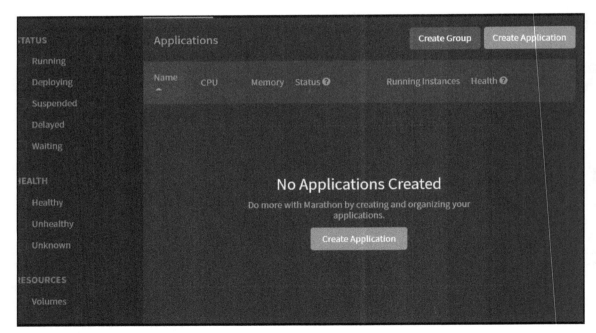

Now we will work on deploying the application on the Mesos cluster. But, before that, we need to perform two most important steps. One is to add information about containerizers, and the other is to add a Marathon user on our slave server. There are multiple types of containerizers, but we will add Docker and Mesos. Mesos is the default one, and we will add Docker as we will run our application inside a Docker container. Docker containerizer allows tasks to be run inside a Docker container, so this is enabled when you configure the agent flag as `containerizer = Docker`. Then we need to add a Marathon user on all our slave servers as, when Marathon deploys the application, it requires a Marathon user on all the slave servers to deploy the application.

1. Now we will enable the containerizer flag, as follows:

```
cd /etc/mesos-slave
pwd
sudo vi containerizers
```

2. Add `mesos`, then `docker` inside the `containerizers` file, and restart the server (`:wq!`), and then restart the Mesos slave server by running the following command:

```
sudo service mesos-slave restart
```

3. Check the status by running the following:

```
sudo service mesos-slave status
```

4. Do the same thing in `slave2`. So, you need to perform these steps on all the servers. Let's add the user. First, we'll check whether we have a Marathon user by running the `id marathon` command; if it's not added, add it by running the `sudo useradd marathon` command. This step needs to be performed on all of the slave servers.

5. Let's deploy a sample application using the Marathon framework to the Mesos cluster. Log in to your Marathon. We will deploy the nginx web server. Click on **Create Application**. Inside the **General** tab, enter any ID you want, CPUs, and disk space as per your requirement. In **Docker Container**, for **Image**, put `nginx`, and **Network** should be **Bridged**. In the **Ports** tab, **Conatainer Port** will be `80`, and **Name** will be `nginx`. Click on **Create Application**. It will start deploying and running. Let's quickly see where it has run that nginx container:

So, it's on `mesos-master2`. So, this is our slave server.

You shouldn't get confused. We have added three master slaves, as well as our Mesos master as a slave.

6. If you click on the ID, it will not connect. The reason behind that is we need to allow the port on AWS, so we need to edit the security group to allow the port. Let's go to the EC2 dashboard. Click on **Security Groups**, click on your security group, which is `mesos1`, then click on **Edit**. We need to add a rule to allow communication on that port and then click on **Save**:

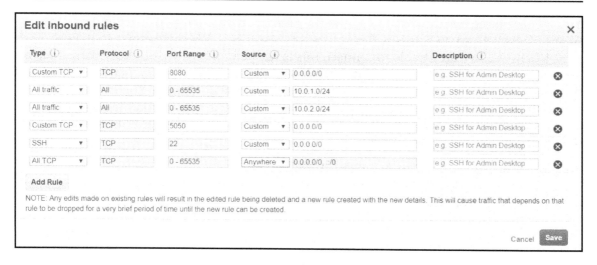

7. We need to add the same thing on another security group (mesos). After this, refresh the page and you will see you have deployed our nginx container successfully and we can access it:

8. So, now we will scale it. On the Marathon where nginx is running, we will click on **Scale Application**, then, in the top-right corner, click on the three dots and select **Scale**. We will make it 3:

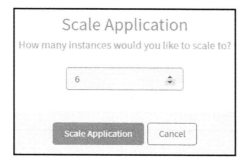

You will see three instances running, and they have run on `mesos-slave2` and `mesos-master1`. So, let's try to access it. Let's try `mesos-master1`. We can connect to it. For `mesos-slave2`, we are unable to connect; this is happening because our host doesn't have a `mesos-slave2` entry. So, we will do the Mesos host entry on our local machine. We'll add the IP, `mesos-slave2`, and save it. If you refresh now, it will connect. You can scale it further if you want, and you can access any instance. So, this is how you can deploy your application in the Mesos cluster and scale it. You can destroy the application by clicking on the three dots and selecting **Destroy**.

We have scaled up and scaled down the nginx container, and now we will see a real-life example where we will run the WordPress container and use the AWS RDS for MySQL database. Let's set up the WordPress container, which connects to the MySQL database. We will be using AWS RDS for MySQL database.

MySQL database on AWS

Let's start with setting up MySQL database on AWS as follows:

1. Go to AWS console, and in the **Database** section click on **Relational Database Service**. Then click on **Get started now**. We need MySQL, so select **MySQL** and click on the **Next** button. In the **Use case** page, select **Dev/Test - MySQL** and click on **Next**:

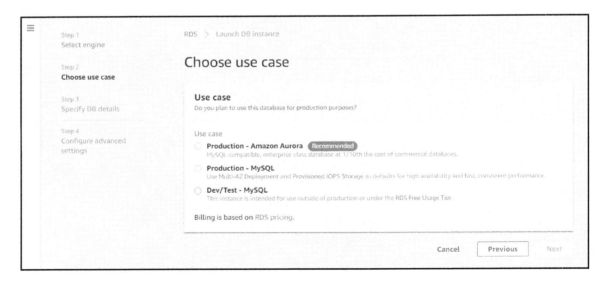

2. Next, in for DB details, select **general-public-license** for the **License model** field, select **mysql 5.6.39** for the DB engine version, select **db.t2.micro** for **DB instance class** field, enter `mesosDatabase` for **DB instance identifier**, then for **Master username**, enter `tetrauser`. Let's provide the DB identifier; we'll use `wordpressmesosdatabase`. Specify the master username, `tetrauser`, and then we need to specify the master password. We will use the master password `tetra1234` and click **Next**.

3. Next, you will see the advanced settings; under the **Network & Security** tab, do the following configuration:

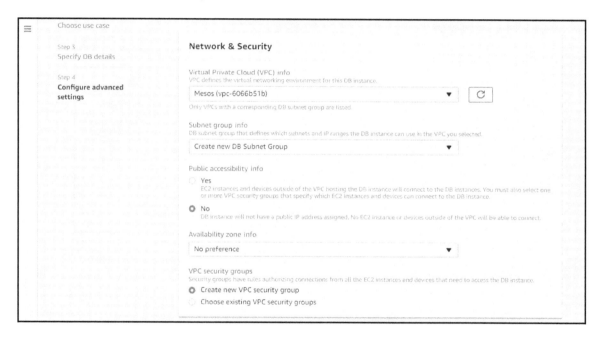

4. For **Database options,** do the following configuration:

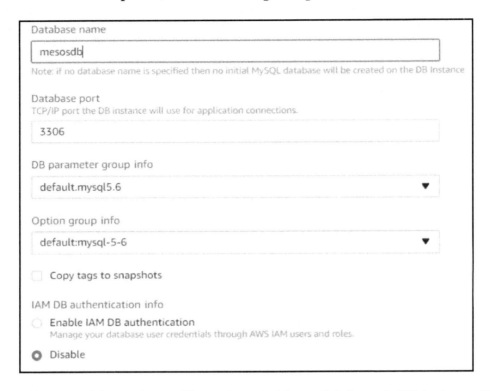

5. The rest of the settings will remain as is. Next, click **Launch DB instance**. Your DB instance will be created. Then click **View DB instance details** to see the DB instance status, which will show **creating**, so wait until it shows **available**:

6. As our database is up and running, let's allow the traffic from our EC2 instances.
   For that, we need the security group that we created. You will find it under
   Details | Security and network | Security groups. Click on it. Under the
   Inbound tab, click **Edit**, do the following settings, and click on **Save**:

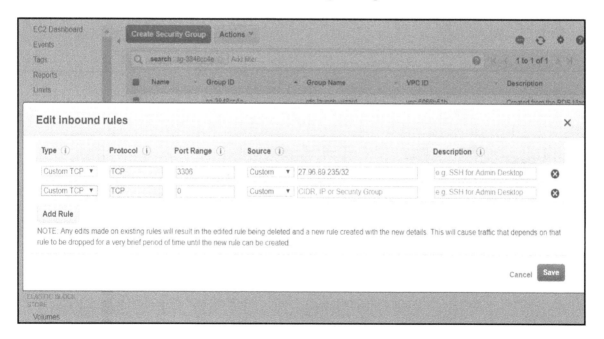

7. This will allow our communication between Mesos EC2 instances to our RDS database. Now we will go on one of the instances and try to telnet on the `3306` port, which will validate if a connection is established or not. To get the URL for our database instance, go to **Relational Database Service** and click on our RDB instance. Under the **Connect** tab, you will find **Endpoint**, which contains a URL:

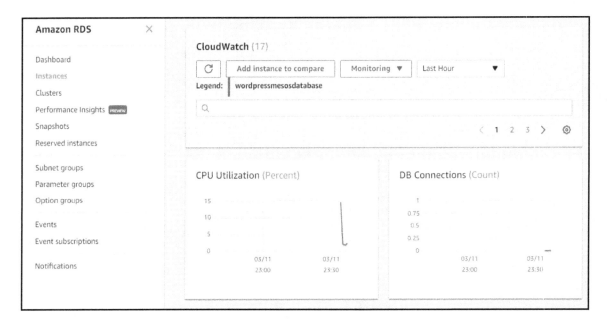

8. Copy the URL, go to our SSH console, and paste it with the `telnet` command:
9. This says we are able to connect to our MySQL successfully on port 3306. Now, deploy our WordPress container on the Mesos cluster using database information. Go to the Marathon load balancer URL, access the Marathon console, and click on **Create Application**. Enter the ID as `wordpress` and the disk space as `500`:

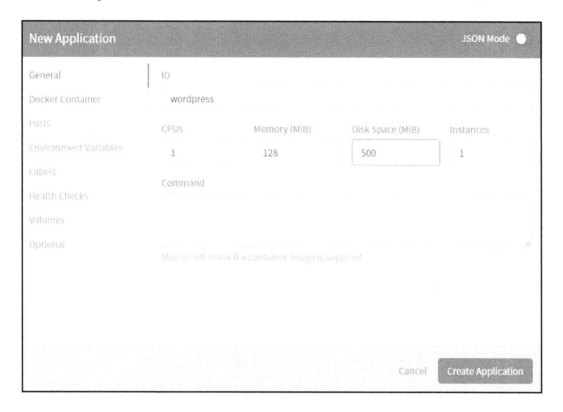

10. The **Docker Container** configuration is as follows:

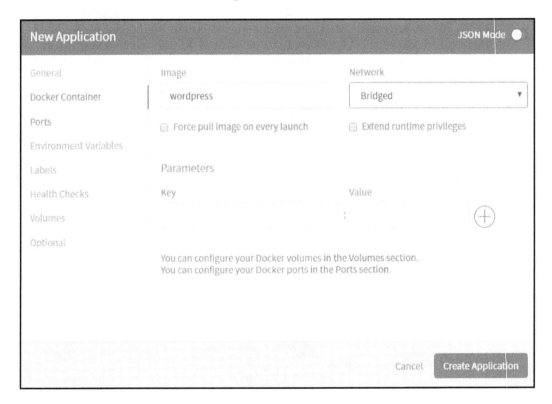

11. Next, the **Ports** configuration is as follows:

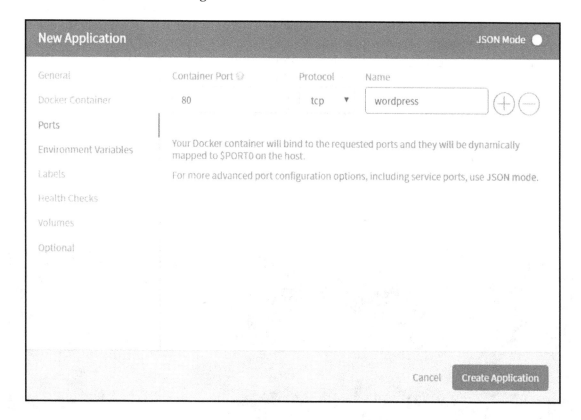

12. We need to provide additional environment variables for WordPress container to connect to a database. So, go to `hub.docker.com` and see how the WordPress container can be set up. We are using an external database, so we need to use the environment variables `WORDPRESS_DB_HOST` or `WORDPRESS_DB_USER` and `WORDPRESS_DB_PASSWORD`. Let's enter `WORDPRESS_DB_HOST` for **Key**, the DNS name and the `8080` port, then add a field and use `WORDPRESS_DB_USER` for **Key**, and `tetrauser` for **Value**. Let's use `WORDPRESS_DB_PASSWORD` for **Key**, and `tetra1234` for **Value**, then click **Create Application**.

I would strongly recommend you use Docker secrets to store your password.

13. The status will show **Deploying**, and then **Running**:

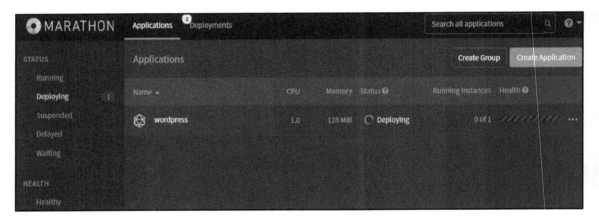

14. Click on `wordpress`, and then click on the ID; it's on `mesos-slave1`. We will not be able to connect. Let's see why. Click on `wordpress` and **Configuration**. So, you see what we have done there; we have given `8080` instead of `3306`:

15. To change the port, go to **Edit**, then **Environment Variables**, and inside **Value**, change it to `3306`:

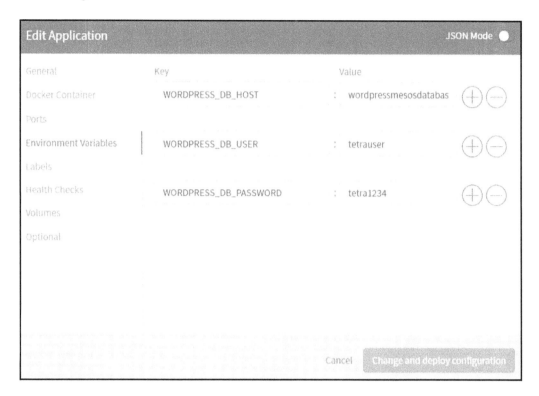

16. Click on **Change and deploy configuration**. Now it will show **Running**; click on `wordpress`, then access the URL.

17. So, we have the install page for your WordPress, and our instance is able to connect to the database successfully. Now we'll stop the database to see what happens to the page. This will help us to verify that our instance is connecting to our database or whether our container is successfully connecting to our database or not. Go to RDS instances and under **Instance actions**, select **Stop**:

So, the database will stop. Now let's try to access it again: it will take time, which means it's trying to connect to the database but it's unable to find it because we have stopped it. So, this proves that we have successfully deployed our WordPress container and it can connect to the database. Let's start the RDS instance again: **Instance actions | Start**. Now the status will be **Starting,** so it will take some time. After we have initiated the start command, we will refresh the page and see whether we get the existing WordPress landing screen again. Our database instance is available now. As you can see, the status is available.

Let's scale up by using **Scale Application**, and scale to 4. You can see it has scaled on different servers, master2, slave1, master3, and slave2. Let's try to validate the URL, by clicking on every instance, and it will show the desired output. Now, one thing comes up here. Do we need to access each master server one by one? How will our customer access it? To resolve this issue, we have Marathon-lb, a service discovery and a load balancing tool for Marathon based on HAProxy. It reads Marathon task information and dynamically generates HAProxy configuration details.

You can see when you scale up an application that it dynamically assigns a `31108` port for each container. You can see this on `slave1`, `master3`, and `slave2` as well. So, what Marathon-lb does is it automatically checks port assignments and makes changes in the configuration so your customer can connect to the newly available services on different ports. That's the advantage of Marathon-lb. So, as soon as the service is available, it discovers that service and it knows on which port it's running, and it makes the changes in the configuration dynamically so our customer can connect to the newly added service. Therefore, to gather the task information, Marathon-lb needs to know where to find Marathon. We will see how to set up the Marathon-lb for service discovery and load balancing to our WordPress container.

Setting up Marathon-lb

First, we should understand why we need Marathon-lb set up. We already deployed a WordPress container in the previous section. So, you have one instance, you know the server name and the port, and, when you click on the link, it will bring up the output page—the WordPress landing page. If you are working on only one instance, then you don't have to use Marathon-lb; you can just have your public IP map to another DNS name and you can access that. In our case, our server is `mesos-master2`, so what we can do is we can just access the `mesos-master2` server on a specific port and then it will get access. You can just configure a load balancer and point to this server on this port and your work is done. In that scenario, you don't need a Marathon-lb setup; you can directly point your AWS Load Balancer to this instance on this specific port and your work is done, but if you're planning to scale your server, you will need Marathon-lb.

Let's scale our application to three instances. If you don't have Marathon-lb then, each time you scale the application, you need to point to another server as well in your load balancer, which is a manual step and time consuming. Currently, we have just added two more instances, but in the real world you might need more than three instances for your application, and you want it to be automatically managed. As soon as the new service comes in, your server or your load balancer should know the server name and the IP address or the server name and port number, and it should get automatically load balanced to that server as well. As soon as your new service arises, it will validate the new service and it will add it in your configuration so your customers can access that server as well. So, the new server is ready to get served, and that's where Marathon-lb comes in very handy to manage your application.

We will see how we will set up the Marathon-lb and then we will see how we can configure HAProxy inside your application. We will use a Docker container for the Marathon-lb set up. We will set up two Docker containers on `marathon1` and `marathon2`, so it's resilient and highly available for us. If either one goes down, the other one will be available to serve the request. Let's run the Docker container. Here is the command to run your Marathon-lb inside the Docker container:

```
$ sudo docker run -d -p 9090:9090 --add-host="mesos-slave1:10.0.1.85" --add-host="mesos-slave2:10.0.1.174"
```

The detached mode is `docker run -d`, and `9090` is the port where HAProxy will bind. So, you can see these ports; we have told HAProxy to use the `9090` port. For access, we will bind the `9090` container port to the `9090` host port, and then we have used a `--add-host` flag. So, this is our Mesos master and slave server. The information will get added in the host file so, in the cluster configuration, HAProxy will know the IP of the server. By using the `--add-host` flag, it will add the name and IP to the host file inside your container. Then we will use the `-e PORTS=9090` environment, which will inform HAProxy to use the `9090` port. We will download this image from Docker Marathon-lb, and then we will give the `--marathon` command. This is again an environment variable to inform HAProxy to use the Marathon UI on this port to fetch the application details. We will be using `sse` mode. In `sse` mode, scripts connect to the Marathon events and point to get notified about state changes. So, that's where, when you deploy the new application, it quickly checks the service detail and makes the changes accordingly, so the new services are ready to be served. Let's press *Enter*:

```
Unable to find image 'mesosphere/marathon-lb:latest' locally
latest: Pulling from mesosphere/marathon-lb
cc20a3251af5: Pull complete
b4e6692eb4b1: Pull complete
a807a2410082: Pull complete
533a024f7c0c: Pull complete
fc9f66b5d6e8: Pull complete
5d36f8939a25: Pull complete
Digest: sha256:a1bd967401686fdc3f86d3c6767e76bd6c79b7f4cce3f0e8a89da766
380e5279
Status: Downloaded newer image for mesosphere/marathon-lb:latest
d6f95d09d2def4986371003a0a5756a5b8713ee8655f0606fb6466a0cfd434fb
[centos@marathon1 ~]$ []
```

The image has been downloaded and it is in the running state now. To validate that, run the following command:

```
$ sudo docker ps -a
```

So, you can see the container ID, image, and command ran inside the container, and you can see the 9090 port is mapped. We will do the same thing in the marathon2 server.

Let's access the HAProxy on the 9090 port:

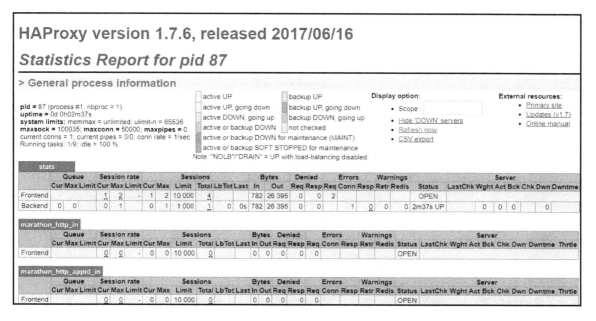

So, this is our marathon1 server on the 9090 port. As you can see, it has started checking the events, and it has started checking the services that are running inside the cluster. So, right now, you know we have scaled the services; it grabbed that information and it is showing it in the preceding output.

So, that's how Marathon-lb works. Now we'll scale one more server and scale it to four, so we have four instances of WordPress. First, let's refresh marathon1. As soon as you have refreshed, you will see the four instances running, so you don't have to worry about adding the configuration manually. So, Marathon-lb using HAProxy detects the new services and makes the changes so your new service is available and ready to get served.

Let's delete this application and see what state we see in the HAProxy console. Go to **Application** and click **Destroy**. Refresh, and then you will see Marathon-lb has detected there are no services running, so all the settings are gone now. So, let's deploy the WordPress application again. We already have our database instance running, so when we deploy our application, it will connect to our database as well. Go to RDS instances and our database instance is available. Let's go to the Marathon console, and again create an application called `wordpress`—what we have already created in the previous section. Let's validate it by clicking on the ID:

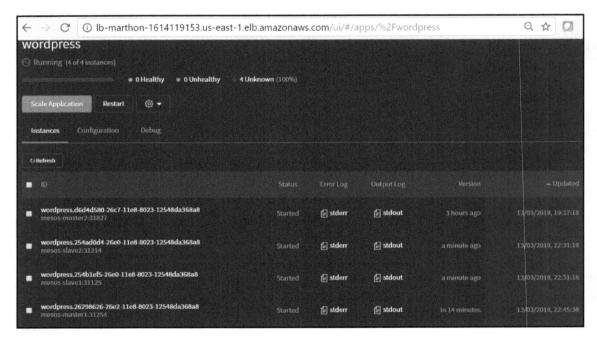

So, you can see the WordPress landing page. If you refresh our HAProxy page, you don't see any information, so you need to understand why this information is not there. We need to define a HAProxy group. So, while starting our instance, we have defined `--group external`. We have defined this while running our Marathon-lb container. We need to define this group in the application. While deploying the application, we need to include a special label with a key HAProxy group, and we have not defined that in our deployment. So, go to **Edit** and change its labels:

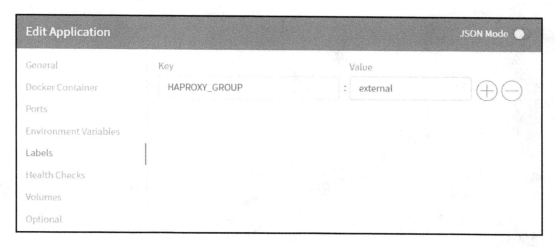

So, this is how, after defining an HAProxy group, Marathon-lb knows which services needs to be exposed:

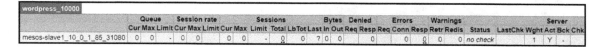

The WordPress container is exposed on port `10000`; HAProxy automatically assigned this port, but there is a way you can control this port as well. Go to the Marathon console, click on **wordpress**, and go **Configuration**. You can change the port as per your requirement. So, let's change it; go to **JSON Mode** and change `servicePort` to `10001`:

```
Edit Application                                                    JSON Mode

 1   {
 2       "id": "/wordpress",
 3       "cmd": null,
 4       "cpus": 1,
 5       "mem": 128,
 6       "disk": 200,
 7       "instances": 1,
 8       "acceptedResourceRoles": [
 9           "*"
10       ],
11       "container": {
12           "type": "DOCKER",
13           "docker": {
14               "forcePullImage": false,
15               "image": "wordpress",
16               "parameters": [],
17               "privileged": false
18           },
19           "volumes": [],
20           "portMappings": [
21               {
22                   "containerPort": 80,
23                   "hostPort": 0,
24                   "labels": {},
25                   "name": "wordpress",
26                   "protocol": "tcp",
27                   "servicePort": 1000
28               }
29           ]
30       },
31       "env": {
```

Refresh the HAProxy page and you can see the port has changed:

So, this port is useful when you run the Marathon-lb container. You need to bind this port to your localhost in the Marathon-lb server. So, as of now, we can directly access the WordPress container using the server name and port, which is defined in our cluster configuration, which you can access to see your page, but our main focus is how we will access all four instances after scaling.

You can't add them each one by one, so you need to have Marathon-lb set up. So, let's quickly set up the configuration for Marathon-lb. We need to bind the 10001 port to our local server in the same way we did when we bound the HAProxy 9090 port to our local server. According to our requirement, you can use whichever port you like, and then you can change the service port in your Marathon UI. We've seen how we changed from 10000 to 10001. First, we will stop the services in marathon1 by running the following command:

```
$ sudo docker ps -a
$ sudo docker stop d6f95d09d2de
```

We will do the same thing on marathon2 server and we will remove this container because we need to run a new container with our port definitions:

```
$ sudo docker ps -a
$ sudo docker stop 5f726bb00028
$ sudo docker rm 5f726bb00028
```

So, now we will run the new container:

```
$ sudo docker run -d -p 9090:9090 -p 8081:10001 --add-host="mesos-
slave:10.0.1.85"
. . .
```

We are putting one more port mapping, which is -p, then the local port you are looking for— 8081—and then 10001. So, you can change the port according to your requirements. If you want to change it to 2, you can do this and then go there in the application configuration and change the service port. So, as of now we'll keep this as 1. Let's validate our server:

```
$ sudo docker ps -a
```

So, you can see our container is running and it has mapped to our localhost on port 8081. Now, we will access the WordPress container via our Marathon-lb. So, let's refresh HAProxy page; as of now, we only have one instance running. Enter `marathon1:8081`. So, you can see we can now access on `marathon1:8081` via Marathon-lb:

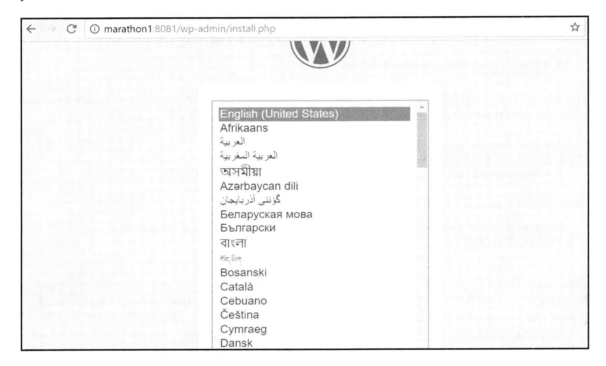

So, we have successfully done our configuration. Let's scale the application, and make it 3, and you will see our two other instances have been started on another server, which are `mesos-slave3` and `mesos-master2`. We can access it by clicking on the IDs. So, let's go via Marathon-lb server and `marathon1:8081`, and you will still have access, so it will load balance on all the three servers. Let's check our HAProxy; you can see the three servers are listed here:

wordpress_10001																							Ser
		Queue			Session rate			Sessions					Bytes		Denied		Errors		Warnings				
	Cur	Max	Limit	Cur	Max	Limit	Cur	Max	Limit	Total	LbTot	Last	In	Out	Req	Resp	Req	Conn	Resp	Retr	Redis	Status	LastChk	Wght	Act
mesos-master2_10_0_1_203_31417	0	0	-	0	2		1	2	-	2	2	9s	2 055	9 462	0		0	0	0		0	no check		1	Y
mesos-master3_10_0_2_68_31849	0	0	-	0	2		2	2	-	2	2	9s	0	0	0		0	0	0		0	no check		1	Y
mesos-slave3_10_0_2_141_31789	0	0	-	0	2		2	2	-	2	2	9s	0	0	0		0	0	0		0	no check		1	Y

So, now it will send a request to all three servers; this is how you can scale your application as per the load. If you can see, on a specific day, that there is a used load or there is any scale going on, you can quickly scale in the application according to your requirements. Now we'll do the same stuff on the `marathon2` server, and you will see you can access the WordPress via `marathon2`.

Now, we will have a Marathon-lb high availability setup. We will use AWS Load Balancer and, as we have done for Mesos and Marathon, we will do the same for Marathon-lb. We will have a load balancer that will point to Marathon-lb on port `8081`. So, now you will load balance `marathon1` and `marathon2` on port `8081`, which is our Marathon-lb via AWS Load Balancer.

So, go to RDS, then go to EC2 instances. Click **Load Balancers**, then **Create Load Balancer**. You will have **Application Load Balancer**. For the **Configure Load Balancer** step, provide the name, `wordpress-lb`. We need **internet-facing**, which will load balance on port `80`, and our **VPC** is **Mesos**. Click both zones and click **Next**. In the **Configure Security Groups** step, create a new security group and name it `wordpress-lb`. The description will be `wordpress load balancer`. Then click **Next**.

Here, we will **Configure Routing**, so we will define **New target group** in **Target group**; we will define our servers, which are `marathon1` and `marathon2`. We'll first name the target group `wordpress-lb`: the port that we want is `8081`, and the target type is `instance`. Then we will click **Next**. In the **Register Targets** step, you need to add `marathon2` and `marathon1` as a target, click **Add to registered**, and click **Next**.

Let's quickly check the **Health checks**; under the **Configuring Routing** step, add 301 and 302 to **Success code**, click **Next**, and then you can click **Create**. So, it will successfully create a load balancer. So, we can see the state is active—that means our load balancer is up and running. Copy the **DNS name** URL:

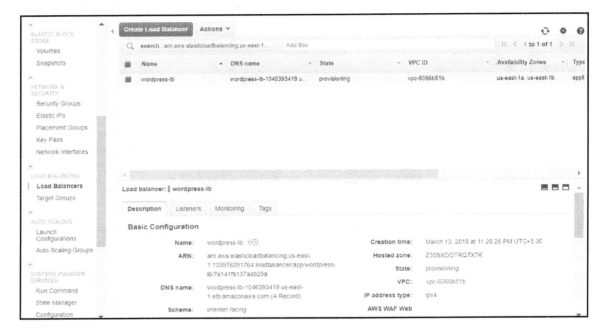

Paste it in the browser. So, you can see the same landing page appears here:

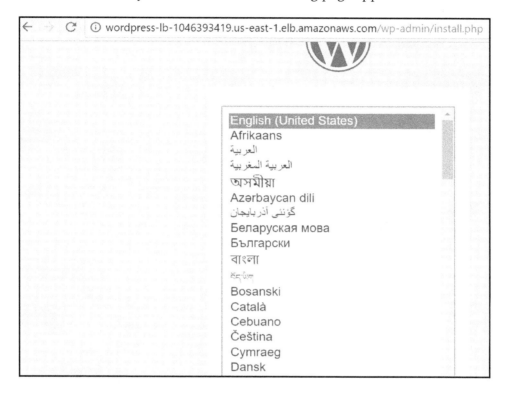

It means our load balancer is forwarding the request to our Marathon-lb, which is inside the Docker container on the `marathon1` and `marathon2` servers. So, let's quickly see the configuration. Go to **Target Groups**, and click `wordpress-lb`. The most important part is we need to see whether our target is healthy or not:

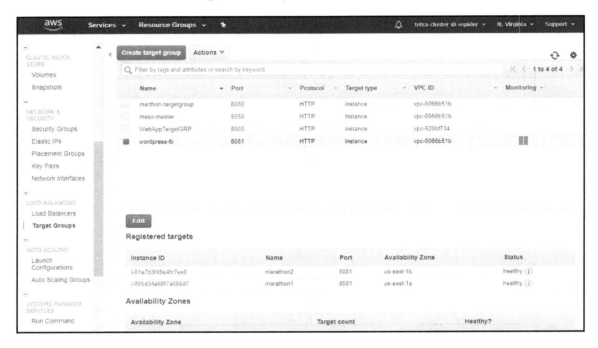

Now we will stop one server, `marathon2`, and see what happens:

```
$ sudo docker ps -a
$ sudo docker stop 7e660e167778
$ sudo docker ps -a
```

Let's validate on the browser. If you refresh it, you will get **502 Bad Gateway**. We need to wait till that instance gets unhealthy, and then our AWS will remove it from the target group. You will see now one of the instances is unhealthy, so if you again refresh the browser, you will see the request will go to another server. Go to **Load Balancers**, then go to **Target Groups**. In **Target Groups**, click `wordpress-lb` and **Health Checks**. In this health check, click **Edit**, and then you can minimize the values, such as making the **Healthy threshold** 2, then you can keep the **Unhealthy threshold** as is, but you can make changes in **Interval** by adding 10, so it will quickly check the service and it will mark it as unhealthy, and it will only show which instances are available. So, that's how you can make changes to quickly bring up the services if one of the instances is down.

Let's stop both instances. Go in `marathon1` and stop this as well using `sudo docker stop, container ID`. Now go to the EC2 console, check the **Targets**—both are unhealthy, so go to browser. So, again, we will get **502 Bad Gateway** because both instances are in an unhealthy state. Let's start one of the Marathon-lb containers again using `sudo docker ps -a`. So, it's up and running. Go to EC2 and refresh this. You can see one of the instances that we started is in a healthy state. Again, go to the browser and refresh, and then you will get the page.

I'm sure Marathon-lb will be useful in your environment.

Summary

We learned how to configure AWS Load Balancer for the Marathon and Mesos master console. AWS Load Balancer helped us to route requests for both the Marathon and all three Mesos master servers. This helped us to ease the management for Mesos and Marathon services. Then, we enabled the containerizer in all of the Mesos slave servers, and we added a Marathon user on all of the slave servers. Both settings are necessary for the deployment of our application on all slaves servers.

Then, we deployed a sample nginx server using the Marathon framework and we saw how you can scale multiple instances very quickly and easily. Then, we took a real-world example where we created an RDS MySQL database for WordPress in AWS, then we deployed a WordPress container in a Mesos cluster and connected a WordPress container to the database.

Then we deployed Marathon-lb, which is based on HAProxy. Marathon-lb is a service discovery tool that is useful when your new service is deployed on your Mesos cluster. It quickly detects that and adds those configurations in the Mesos-lb configuration, and makes the services available for customers; it does everything automatically, and there's no need for manual intervention there. So, once you scale your services, the Marathon-lb HAProxy will detect that and add those configurations and make those services available for your customers. We deployed two Marathon-lb servers, which were load balanced using AWS Load Balancer, so we achieved high availability and resilience there as well. In the next chapter, we will learn about persistent volumes and how to use it in Docker.

6
Persistent Volumes

The Mesos agent component, containerizer, is responsible for running the tasks/services within the containers. This avails you with lot of benefits, from isolating a task from the other running tasks for avoiding any conflicts between them to controlling the overall task's resource usage programmatically.

Here, we will understand what the containerizer is. This section briefly introduces the concept of containers, and also provides a detailed overview of the following different containerization options in Mesos:

- Contain tasks to run in a limited-resource runtime environment
- Control a task's resource usage, such as CPU and memory, programmatically
- Run software in the prepackaged filesystem image, allowing it to run in different environments

Let's understand the different types of containers and containerizers that we have. Mesos implements the following containerizers:

- **Composing**: This feature helps in multiple container technology in one shot. When you configure the `--containerizers` agent flag with the multiple comma-separated containerizer name, this container is enabled in our environment. So, let's quickly see our configuration file in which we have enabled the containerizers. You need to go inside the slave server by navigating to the `cd /etc/mesos` file to enable your containerizer technology. Here we have enabled Mesos and Docker, which play together to run the containers.
- **Docker**: This is one of the most popular technology containerizers and it allows tasks to run inside a Docker container, which is enabled by configuring the agent flag as `--containerizers=docker`.
- **Mesos**: This native containerizer allows tasks to be run with an array of pluggable isolaters provided by Mesos, and is enabled on configuring the agent flag as `--containerizers=mesos`.

Later, you will see how to run the container images to run the container in our slave servers using the Marathon framework to schedule and execute the containers on the slave server with the help of Mesos cluster, which manages all our containers. I hope this will help you to deploy containers in your environment. Before we go ahead with containerizer, we will be learning about the advantages and limitations of persistent volumes. We will also be creating a demo to know more about persistent volumes using EBS persistent volumes in AWS.

In this chapter we will cover the following topics:

- What is persistent volumes
- The need for persistent volumes
- How to use persistent volumes using Docker

Introduction to persistent volumes

To understand persistent volumes, first we need to understand the following stateless and stateful applications:

- **Stateless**: With stateless applications, the application does some calculations based on one or more input and sends its results to one or more output. When the application is run on such data, it will do the same job. Usually these types of applications scale very well and are easier to write and maintain.
- **Stateful**: The stateful application is one that needs to store data, so databases are the best example of stateful applications. A database is a special type of application in which we store the data of our system, which is then stored on disk. In Mesos, on the completion or failure of tasks, all data created by these tasks could be deleted. For example, if one of the applications storing the customer information in the database is lost, terminated, or shut down but state, the database remains the same if you are using persistent volumes. If you are not using persistent volumes, your data will be lost. So, for stateful applications, you should have a persistent volume for the database where your data will get stored and can be retrieved later on if any of the application gets terminated.
- **There are two ways to handle the problem**: You can use the shared filesystem or the persistent volumes.

Need for persistent volumes

The idea behind persistent volumes is quite easy; the application can reserve some space for specific tasks and mark them as persistent volumes. When the application that is using this space terminates, the newly spawned application will get access to the data created by the previously-terminated application so they can restore the data. We can have a shared filesystem or we can have persistent volumes, as these are the only two ways to handle the problem.

Here, we will use EBS persistent volumes in AWS to understand how our data will be persisted on the EBS volume using the REX-Ray volume driver. The following procedure illustrates the problem of why we need persistent volumes:

1. We will run the Redis Docker image from Marathon to deploy on the Mesos slave server, which will save Redis data to a local Docker volume. We will save some data on Redis using the Redis command.
2. We cease Docker on the server where the Redis container is running, which will automatically detect the issue and re-run on another server. This means Mesos is notified that something is going wrong (the Redis container is not reachable), and hence it will re-run on another server.
3. We will check with the accessibility of the original container's data to understand it more clearly.

Before getting into the practical aspect of how you will perform persistent volume configuration, first we will look at the consequences of not using the persistent volumes. So, let's perform a quick demo here.

1. As shown in the following screenshot of our Marathon server, we will run the image by clicking on the **Create Application** button and providing the following required details:
   - **ID**: redis-test
   - **CPUs**: 0.2
   - **Memory (MiB)**: 50

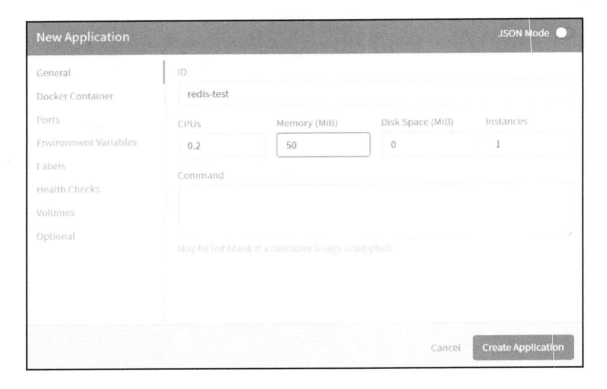

2. In the left navigation pane, click on the **Docker Container** pane and type `redis` under the **Image** option:

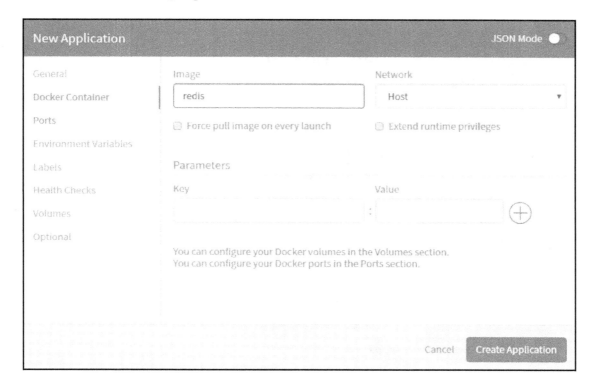

3. Then, click on the **Environment Variables** pane and fill in the following fields:
   - **Key**: `volume`
   - **Value**: `redis_vol:/tmp`

4. Click on the **Create Application** button. Now, you can see that `mesos-master2.server` is running:

5. The reason why it's run on mesos-master2 is that a Mesos slave is enabled on the master server, so we can have a number of slave servers. So, let's quickly log into the master2 server, to check the Redis process by executing the following command line:

```
sudo docker ps -a
```

6. You can see our Redis container is running here:

7. Now, we will enter into this Redis container and save some data by executing the following command line:

```
sudo docker exec -it 9ff330e78c79 redis-cli
```

8. Let's save some data and exit:

```
127.0.0.1:6379> set data loca_Data
OK1
127.0.0.1:6379> save
OK
127.0.0.1:6379> exit
```

9. Let's try to get data that we saved earlier to understand whether we can get this saved data after running another container on the server:

```
127.0.0.1:6379> get data
"loca_Data"
127.0.0.1:6379>
```

10. So, what we are going to do here is stop the Docker container or process that we already ran on mesos-master2 by executing the following command line:

```
sudo service docker stop
```

11. You can see the following output:

```
Redirecting to /bin/systemctl stop docker.service
```

12. Let's go to Marathon console. You can see in the following screenshot that it has detected the issue and it is running on another server now, which is `mesos-slave1`:

13. Let's quickly log into the `mesos-slave1` server and see whether we can get that data of the container ID:

    ```
    $ sudo docker ps -a
    ```

14. Remember to change the container ID every time you hit the `exec` command to get data from the volumes. As you can see, it says `(nil)`, so it has not found the data:

    ```
    $ sudo docker exec -it 1e34d10e43f9 redis-cli
    127.0.0.1:6379>
    127.0.0.1:6379> get data
    (nil)
    127.0.0.1:6379>
    ```

This means, along with the creation of a container on another server, the local volume got created on the local server, which disabled the access to the data created on our `master2` server.

Now we understood why persistent volumes are necessary for our stateful applications. In the preceding example, we started a Redis container with Redis volume using Marathon to deploy on a Mesos slave. The Redis image failed to get the volume from the old node and instead it created a new Redis volume on a new server, which disabled the access to the created data.

Let's see the following limitations of Redis:

- **Lack of external storage support**: By default, Docker stores all the volumes in the `var/lib/docker` directory, which can become an obstacle to its capacity and performance. Failure of the host might lead to the loss of data, disabling the data retrieval.
- **Data persistency**: Docker data volumes are not globally persistent. The mobility of a Docker container from one physical host to another or the failure of the running Docker container in the node decides the persistency of the Docker volume.

Volume persistent using Docker

In this section we will see how we can make the volume persistent in our Mesos environment that is using Docker by using **REX-Ray.**

Rex-Ray is a storage-orchestration tool that provides a set of common commands for managing multiple storage platforms. It's built on top of the lib storage 6 framework. REX-Ray enables persistent storage for container runtimes such as Docker and Mesos. The following image shows, that we have a REX-Ray installed on each of the Docker hosts and we have a storage platform:

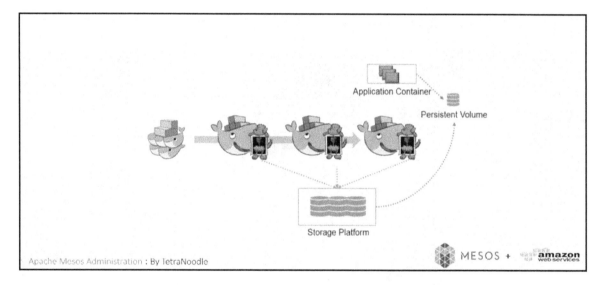

In our case, the storage platform we will have is our **Elastic Block Storage** (EBS), which can be found in AWS. We will use the already-created persistent volume to mount it in the application container, and we will perform the same step we performed in the previous example to understand whether our data remains persistent.

1. Let's get started by first by installing REX-Ray on an AWS instance where we have a Docker container so that Docker provides the plugin to install REX-Ray:

```
sudo docker plugin install rexray/ebs EBS_ACCESSKEY={ACCESSKEY}
EBS_SECRETKEY={SECRET_KEY}
```

2. You need to enter the your ESS access key and secret key you acquired from AWS. You will get the following output:

```
Plugin "rexray/ebs" is requesting the following privileges:
 - network: [host]
 - mount: [/dev]
 - allow-all-devices: [true]
 - capabilities: [CAP_SYS_ADMIN]
Do you grant the above permissions? [y/N] y
latest: Pulling from rexray/ebs
0bf0eb32c628: Download complete
Digest: sha256:a54e6ab53424f5921a713d14af62545a4b98c0efb6c0938076531050f38aed4f
Status: Downloaded newer image for rexray/ebs:latest
Installed plugin rexray/ebs
[centos@mesos-master2 mesos-slave]$
[centos@mesos-master2 mesos-slave]$
[centos@mesos-master2 mesos-slave]$
[centos@mesos-master2 mesos-slave]$
[centos@mesos-master2 mesos-slave]$
[centos@mesos-master2 mesos-slave]$
[centos@mesos-master2 mesos-slave]$
[centos@mesos-master2 mesos-slave]$
[centos@mesos-master2 mesos-slave]$
[centos@mesos-master2 mesos-slave]$
[centos@mesos-master2 mesos-slave]$
[centos@mesos-master2 mesos-slave]$
[centos@mesos-master2 mesos-slave]$
[centos@mesos-master2 mesos-slave]$
[centos@mesos-master2 mesos-slave]$
[centos@mesos-master2 mesos-slave]$
[centos@mesos-master2 mesos-slave]$
[centos@mesos-master2 mesos-slave]$
```

In the preceding screenshot, you can see it is plugging and `rexray/ebs` is requesting the following privileges. Type *y* to grant the permission and hit the *Enter* button. This will pull `rexray` and install it.

3. Now just clear the screen and execute the following command line to validate the Docker volume:

   ```
   sudo docker volume ls
   ```

   The preceding command line will generate the following output:

   ```
   DRIVER                 VOLUME NAME
   local                  6dbb39063a3e6ddb66dcc8be0362d70db68fda5cc81d1f6268eb02dca756ffc7
   local                  b7ae8e5ee8c35eb59cd83cdb5a87de7400b18e7c1a3c2899c829dc97e89747e8
   [centos@mesos-master2 mesos-slave]$ sudo docker plugin ls
   ID                     NAME              DESCRIPTION             ENABLED
   0da7cb453fee           rexray/ebs:latest REX-Ray for Amazon EBS  true
   ```

   As of now, you don't see any volume with our REX-Ray plugin, but you can see your plugin details here. Here you will see your REX-Ray for Amazon EBS is enabled, so we will do the same thing on all other servers.

4. Let's quickly validate our REX-Ray plugin by executing the following command line:

   ```
   sudo docker plugin ls
   ```

5. You you see it is enabled on `slave1` as well as `slave2`.

6. Now, let's run the Redis container on our Mesos slave servers using Marathon and deploy the Redis container using the persistent volume. Click on the **Create Application** button and select the **General** pane to fill in the following fields:

- **ID**: redis
- **CPUs**: 0.2
- **Memory (MiB)**: 50

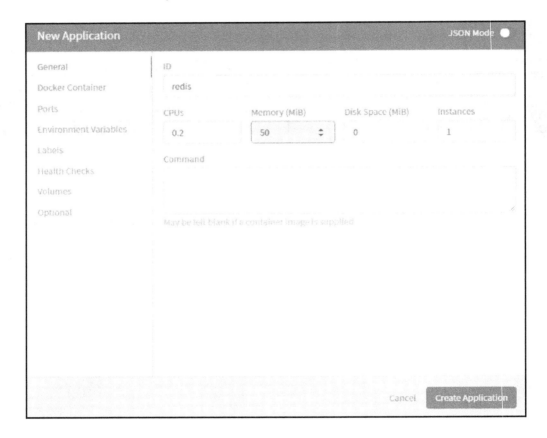

7. Click on the **Docker Container** pane and fill in the following fields:
    - **Image**: **redis**.
    - **Host**: **Bridged**.
    - **Parameters**: We will add two keys here. First, type `volume-driver` under the **Key** field and enter the `rexray/ebs` value under the **Value** option. To add one more parameter here, click on the plus sign and type volume under the **Key** option, and then enter the `vol_redis:/data` value under the **Value** field:

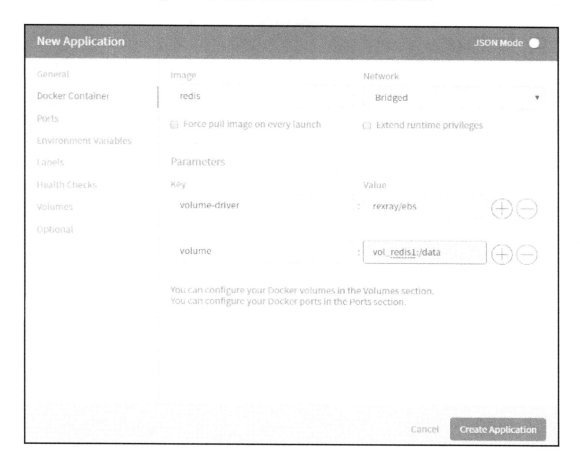

8. Now click on the **Create Application** button. You will see it's deploying:

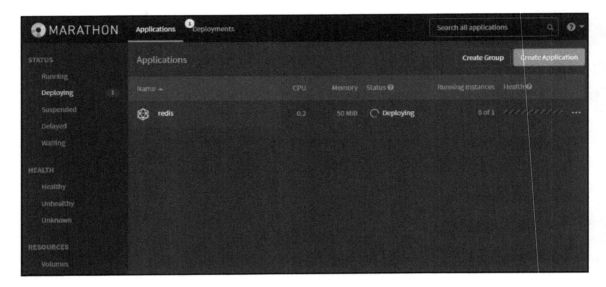

9. Let's quickly go to our EC2 management console. Refresh here, and then you will see our volume is created:

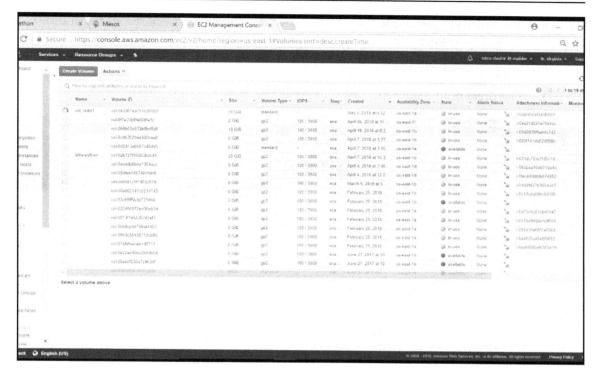

10. So, let's wait for volume to be created, and then your Redis container will come in running state, in `mesos-slave1`:

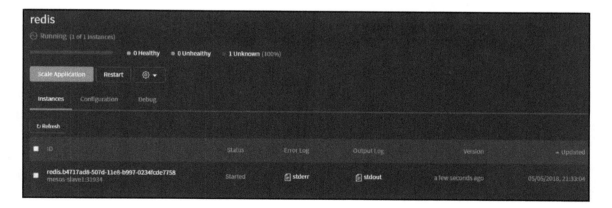

11. Let's quickly jump into the `mesos-slave1` server and check the status of our process by executing the following command line:

```
sudo docker ps -a
```

The preceding command line will generate the following output:

```
INER ID        IMAGE               COMMAND                CREATED              STATUS
RTS                                NAMES
e561754        redis               "docker-entrypoint.s…"  About a minute ago   Up 28 seconds
79/tcp, 0.0.0.0:31934->31934/tcp   mesos-8f4105e7-6887-45ce-9709-26de49b7154e
os@mesos-slave1 ~]$
```

12. Let's enter our container ID, which is `23874`, by executing the following command line:

```
sudo docker exec -it 23874e561754 redis-cl
```

13. Now we will set the data here and hit *Enter*, as shown earlier. `save` and `exit` the container:

```
127.0.0.1:6379> set data persistent_ata
127.0.0.1:6379> save
127.0.0.1:6379> exit
```

14. We will stop our Docker process here and Mesos will be notified about the failure, and then it will run this container on another node. Take a look at the following snippet:

```
$ sudo service docker stop
connecting to /bin/systemctl stop docker.service
```

15. As you can see in the following screenshot, as soon as the process is stopped, it tries to migrate on the `mesos-slave2` server. Let's wait until it comes into running state:

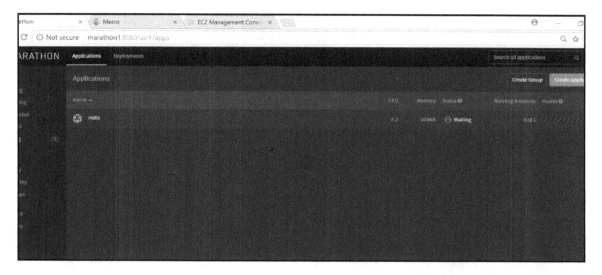

16. So, here you can see it's in running state now:

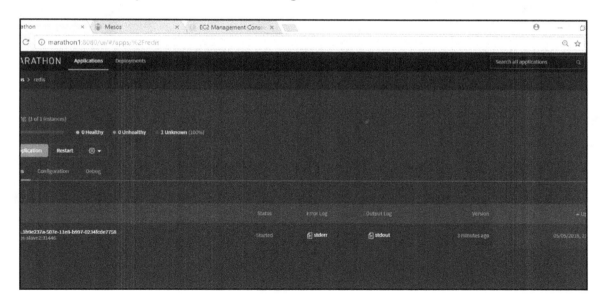

17. Let's jump into the `mesos-slave2` server. As you can see in the following screenshot, our Redis container has started on the `mesos-slave2` server:

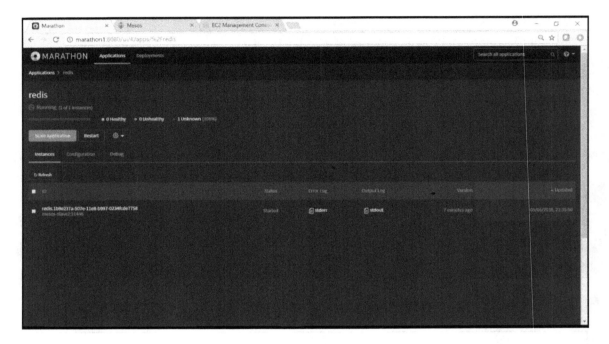

18. Let's check the process that got migrated from `slave1` to `slave2` by executing the following command line:

```
sudo docker ps -a
```

19. Perform the following `exec` command to enter the container:

```
sudo docker exec -it 0545be937c65 redis-cli
```

20. Run the following command, and then you can see that the persistent data information is available once the container gets migrated to another server:

```
get data
```

The preceding command line will generate the following output:

```
"persistent_data"
127.0.0.1:6379>
```

So, this is how the REX-Ray volume driver can be used to make your volume persistent across nodes and containers.

In this example, we started a Redis container with `redis_vol` on the server using Marathon. On another node, the Redis image successfully attaches to the existing volume, making data persistent across the nodes.

Now, let's explore the advantages:

- **Persistent Docker data**: We get persistent Docker data using our Mesos configuration and environment with Marathon. The container data is stored on EBS volumes using the REX-Ray volume driver, making it globally persistent, which is useful during containers' migration as well.
- **Container migration**: Containers can be migrated from one host to another without losing access to the data that has a failover support.
- **Failover support**: An automatic failure of a container over to a different host provides access to the container data, and we retrieve our data using the persistent volume.

Summary

In this chapter, we learned about stateless and stateful applications, and the different advantages and limitations of using persistent volumes. We also saw how to use the persistent volume in AWS and Docker using Redis and REX-Ray.

In the next chapter, we will be learning more about securing Mesos using authentication.

7
Securing Mesos

Let's secure Mesos by using authentication. In this chapter, we will learn how to authenticate agents to prevent unknown agents and frameworks from joining the cluster. To prevent the launch of unauthorized frameworks, we can specify a secret that needs to be passed by the framework to be accepted by Mesos. The Scheduler API accepts the principal and the secret as a way of authenticating frameworks. The same approach applies to agents as well. Only those knowing the secret can join the cluster. So before we work on configuring authentication, we have to identify the principals of our cluster and generate secrets for them. In the example presented in this chapter, we will assume we have two principals: `marathon1` (framework), and `agent` (all agents).

The following topics will be covered in this chapter:

- Enabling and configuring authentication
- Configuring agents
- Enabling secured socket layer security

Enabling and configuring authentication

Before anything else, we need to enable authentication, and for doing this, we need to define which authentication mechanism we want to use. Here, we will be using CRAM-MD5 because it is built into Mesos and is a popular authentication algorithm used in **Simple Mail Transfer Protocol (SMTP)** and **Lightweight Directory Access Protocol (LDAP)**.

We will work on the following:

- **Master**: This will enable the authentication of frameworks and agents.
- **Agent**: We will create a file with the agent's secrets and this file will be used to authenticate the master.
- **Marathon**: This accepts credentials in a different manner to Mesos. Instead of storing everything in one file, only secrets are stored in the file. We can pass this principal using the command-line flag.

Enabling authentication

We will enable authentication and frameworks by setting `authenticate_frameworks=true` and `authenticate_agents=true`. To do this, follow these steps:

1. Authenticate the agents and framework:

```
$   cd /etc/mesos-master
$ sudo touch authenticate_frameworks
$ sudo touch authenticate_agents
```

2. Create the files:

```
$ Sudo vi authenticate_frameworks
```

3. You should see the following on your screen:

4. Insert `true`, and exit the file with `:wq!`

Repeat these steps for all master servers. We have now enabled the authentication by setting frameworks and agents as true in all the master servers.

Choosing authenticators

We have chosen our authenticator as CRAM-MD5; it is a widely-used algorithm in authentication, and is also a built-in algorithm in Mesos. The following steps show how can this be chosen using the command-line:

1. Choose the authenticator as CRAM-MD5 by running the following commands:

```
$ sudo touch authenticators
$ sudo vi authenticators
```

2. Insert `crammd5` and exit with `:wq!`

Repeat the preceding steps for all the Moses master servers.

Creating a file with a principal secret

The secrets provided will be used in authentication. The current information will be checked against this principal secret file to give authentication.

For creating a secret, let's follow these steps:

1. Create a configuration directory:

```
$ sudo mkdir conf
```

2. In `conf` directory, create a file, `credentials.json`:

```
$ sudo vi credentials.json
```

3. Add the following code to `credentials.json` file:

```
{
    "credentials":
    [
        {
            "principal": "marathon",
            "secret": "marathon1_secret"
        },
        {
            "principal":"agent",
            "secret":"agents_secret"
        }
    ]
}
```

Save the file using :wq!, and then exit. Repeat these steps on all three master servers.

Credential files, as their name suggests, should be given minimum access, so let's change the permission of our credential file:

1. In the **mesos** tab, key in the following commands:

   ```
   $ sudo chmod 600 /etc/mesos-master/conf/credentials.json
   ```

2. Go to the master's tabs, insert the same command, and type the following:

   ```
   $ ls -rlt
   ```

3. Try appending the following into the credentials.json file:

   ```
   $ sudo cat credentials.json
   ```

You should see the contents of the file, but you won't be able to add anything. Hence our credential.json file is now secured with the 600 permission.

We will need to let the master know about the location of the credential file. We will do this by running some commands in the **mesos** tab:

1. Return to the mesos-master directory and type the following:

   ```
   $ sudo touch credentials
   $ sudo vi credentials
   ```

2. Insert /etc/mesos-master/conf/credentials.json, save, and exit.
3. Repeat the preceding steps for all the master servers.
4. Let's not keep the credential file in conf directory. Instead, let's place it in the /etc/mesos/master directory. Key in the following for all the master servers:

   ```
   $ sudo mv credentials /etc/mesos-master/
   ```

5. Copy the /etc/mesos master/conf/credentials.json path and place it in the file of the credential for each master.

We have now informed the master about the location of the credential file.

Configuring agents

To configure agents, follow these steps:

1. In the **slaves** tab, type the following commands:

```
$ cd /etc/mesos-slave
$ sudo mkdir conf
```

2. Repeat this for all the agents.
3. In the `conf` directory, create a `credential.json` file for all agents:

```
$ cd conf
$ sudo touch credential.json
$ sudo vi credential.json
```

4. Add the following code in the `credential.json` file:

```
{
        "principal": "agent",
        "secret": "agents_secret"
}
```

5. Save and exit using `:wq!`

This is the secret that the agents will use to get authenticated by the master. We added similar secrets for the master previously. The master will now know what secrets to use to get authenticated.

Repeat the preceding steps for all the agents.

The following steps will notify the master about the location of the credential file:

1. These steps are similar to what we followed for the master:

```
$ sudo touch credential
$ cd conf/
$ pwd
//Copy the path that appears as the output of the above command.
```

It should be something like `/etc./mesos-slave/conf`. Paste it and append to it `/credential.json` file.

2. Return to the `mesos- slave` directory by using the `cd. .` command.
3. Open the `$ sudo vi credential.json` credential file.
4. Insert the following path:

   /etc/mesos-slave/conf/credential.json

Save and exit using `:wq!`, and repeat the preceding steps for all agents.

We have successfully configured the agents. We will now move onto Marathon!

Configuring Marathon

Marathon is a control system that can be used in Docker or in cgroups containers, and is cluster wide. It is a framework for Apache Mesos that helps you manage tasks through RESTful APIs.

Let's go back to the Marathon tab and follow these steps:

1. Add a secret to the `marathon` file:

   ```
   $ cd /etc/marathon
   ```

2. Go inside `/etc/default` and:

   ```
   $ sudo touch mesos_authentication_secret
   $ sudo vi mesos
   ```

3. Insert `marathon1_secret`, save the file, and exit using `:wq!`
4. Inform Marathon about the location of the credential file in the **marathon1** tab:

   ```
   $ sudo mkdir conf
   $ sudo cd conf
   $ sudo touch mesos_authentication_secret_file
   $ ll /etc/default/mesos
   $ ll /etc/default/mesos_authentication_secret
   ```

5. You will get a path, `/etc/default/mesos_authentication_secret`. Copy this path.
6. Go to the `conf` directory:

   ```
   $ cd conf/
   $ sudo vi authentication_secret_file
   ```

7. Paste the path that you copied. Save and exit using :wq!.

8. Restart Marathon and check whether you are able to view the configuration in process:

   ```
   $ sudo service marathon stop
   ```

9. Check the status:

   ```
   $ sudo service marathon status
   $ sudo service marathon status -l
   ```

10. You should see the following:

As you can see, we are not able to view the Marathon service that we configured, so we will have to explicitly specify it. To do this, follow these steps:

1. Visit `marathon.service` and specify what we need:

   ```
   $ ps -ef |grep marathon
   ```

   You should see the following:

2. Remember how we configured this? We will repeat the same thing here:

   ```
   $ history |grep marathon.service
   ```

3. The following is what you should see on your screen:

```
marathon1  marathon2  mesos  master2  master3  slave1  slave2  slave3
   73  vi marathon.service
   74  sudo vi marathon.service
   91  vi marathon.service
  116  vi marathon.service
  117  sudo vi marathon.service
  143  vi marathon.service
  144  sudo vi marathon.service
  649  find / -name marathon.service
  651  sudo find . -name marathon.service
  652  vi ./system/multi-user.target.wants/marathon.service
  660  find . -name marathon.service
  661  find / -name marathon.service
  662  sudo find / -name marathon.service
  663  cp /etc/systemd/system/multi-user.target.wants/marathon.service /tmp/marathon.service.bak
  664  vi /etc/systemd/system/multi-user.target.wants/marathon.service
  689  sudo vi marathon.service
  711  sudo vi marathon.service
  713  sudo vi marathon.service
  775  cat marathon.service
  777  vi marathon.service
  778  sud vi marathon.service
  779  sudo vi marathon.service
  847  cat /tmp/marathon.service.bak
  879  find / -name marathon.service
  881  sudo vi /etc/systemd/system/multi-user.target.wants/marathon.service
  883  sudo vi /etc/systemd/system/multi-user.target.wants/marathon.service
  918  sudo vi /etc/systemd/system/multi-user.target.wants/marathon.service
 1055  sudo vi /etc/systemd/system/multi-user.target.wants/marathon.service
 1067  history |grep marathon.service
[centos@marathon1 conf]$
```

4. Go into the system and edit the `marathon.service` file:

```
$ sudo vi
/etc/systemd/system/multi-0user.target.wants/marathon.service
```

You will see a file that we will edit:

5. Beside `e=marathon`, type the following:

```
--
mesos_authentication_secret_file=/etc/default/mesos_authentication_
secret
```

Save and exit using `:wq!`.

6. Type `$ sudo service marathon stop`, and you should see the following:

As you can see, we first need to run the `systemct1` daemon reload once we change the service file. Hence, `$ systemct1 daemon-reload`, `$ sudo service marathon stop`, and `$ sudo service marathon start`. Now check the status:

```
$ sudo service marathon status -1
```

7. Hence, we can see that we have successfully enabled our secret file:

```
/ch.qos.logback.logback-core-1.2.3.jar:/usr/share/marathon/lib/com.wix.accord-core_2.12-0.7.1.jar:/usr/
share/marathon/lib/com.google.inject.guice-4.1.0.jar:/usr/share/marathon/lib/com.fasterxml.jackson.modu
le.jackson-module-scala_2.12-2.8.9.jar:/usr/share/marathon/lib/io.kamon.kamon-system-metrics_2.12-0.6.7
.jar:/usr/share/marathon/lib/org.slf4j.log4j-over-slf4j-1.7.21.jar:/usr/share/marathon/lib/com.sun.jers
ey.jersey-server-1.18.6.jar:/usr/share/marathon/lib/io.netty.netty-codec-http-4.0.43.Final.jar:/usr/sha
re/marathon/lib/org.hdrhistogram.HdrHistogram-2.1.9.jar:/usr/share/marathon/lib/org.jboss.logging.jboss
-logging-3.2.1.Final.jar:/usr/share/marathon/lib/org.eclipse.jetty.jetty-servlets-9.3.6.v20151106.jar:/
usr/share/marathon/lib/com.sun.jersey.contribs.jersey-multipart-1.18.6.jar:/usr/share/marathon/lib/org.
eclipse.jetty.jetty-server-9.3.6.v20151106.jar:/usr/share/marathon/lib/org.aspectj.aspectjrt-1.8.13.jar
:/usr/share/marathon/lib/org.slf4j.jcl-over-slf4j-1.7.21.jar:/usr/share/marathon/lib/org.eclipse.jetty.
jetty-util-9.3.6.v20151106.jar:/usr/share/marathon/lib/com.github.spullara.mustache.java.compiler-0.9.0
.jar:/usr/share/marathon/lib/com.google.protobuf.protobuf-java-3.5.0.jar:/usr/share/marathon/lib/javax.
activation.activation-1.1.jar:/usr/share/marathon/lib/io.kamon.kamon-jmx_2.12-0.6.7.jar:/usr/share/mara
thon/lib/org.asynchttpclient.async-http-client-2.0.25.jar:/usr/share/marathon/lib/org.apache.curator.cu
rator-client-4.0.0.jar:/usr/share/marathon/lib/io.netty.netty-codec-4.0.43.Final.jar:/usr/share/maratho
n/lib/com.google.code.findbugs.jsr305-3.0.0.jar:/usr/share/marathon/lib/com.googlecode.libphonenumber.l
ibphonenumber-6.2.jar:/usr/share/marathon/lib/org.apache.httpcomponents.httpclient-4.5.2.jar:/usr/share
/marathon/lib/com.fasterxml.jackson.jaxrs.jackson-jaxrs-json-provider-2.8.9.jar:/usr/share/marathon/lib
/org.eclipse.jetty.jetty-http-9.3.6.v20151106.jar:/usr/share/marathon/lib/com.google.inject.extensions.
guice-servlet-4.1.0.jar:/usr/share/marathon/lib/io.reactivex.rxscala_2.12-0.26.5.jar:/usr/share/maratho
n/lib/com.papertrail.profiler-1.0.2.jar:/usr/share/marathon/lib/com.fasterxml.classmate-1.1.0.jar mesos
phere.marathon.Main --master zk://10.0.1.42:2181,10.0.1.203:2181,10.0.2.68:2181/mesos --zk zk://10.0.1.
42:2181,10.0.1.203:2181,10.0.2.68:2181/marathon --hostname=marathon1 --mesos_role=marathon --mesos_auth
entication_secret_file=/etc/default/mesos_authentication_secret

May 06 10:55:06 marathon1 systemd[1]: Starting Scheduler for Apache Mesos...
May 06 10:55:06 marathon1 systemd[1]: Started Scheduler for Apache Mesos.
May 06 10:55:06 marathon1 marathon[2727]: No start hook file found ($HOOK_MARATHON_START). Proceeding w
ith the start script.
[centos@marathon1 conf]$
```

8. Also, you can see all services running:

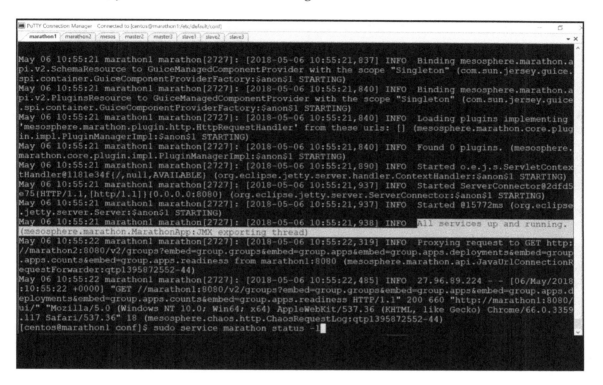

9. Go to the **slave1** tab and restart the agent:

```
$ sudo vi credential
$ sudo service mesos-slave restart
$ sudo service mesos-slave status
```

10. Check the status of the slave that we restarted:

```
$ sudo service mesos-slave status
```

11. If it shows failure, check the log:

```
$ cd /var/log/mesos
```

You will see something such as follows:

12. Copy the latest log and open that file using the `vi` command. You may get the following listing on the file:

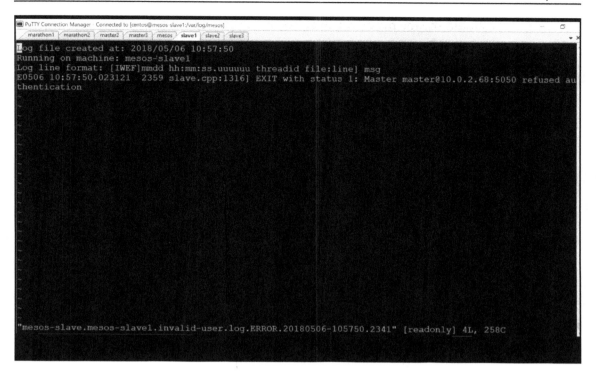

You can see in the preceding screenshot that we have an authentication error. Hence, let's first stop all the slaves by typing $ sudo service mesos-slave stop.

13. Restart the master by going on the **mesos** tab:

```
$ sudo service mesos-master restart
```

Do this for all the masters. Check the status of the masters:

```
$ sudo service mesos-master status -l
```

14. You should see the master in an active running state:

```
 marathon1   marathon2   master2   master3   mesos   slave1   slave2   slave3
May 06 10:59:39 mesos mesos-master[1369]: I0506 10:59:39.489774  1375 master.cpp:7359] Ignoring ...nges
May 06 10:59:44 mesos mesos-master[1369]: I0506 10:59:44.832376  1375 master.cpp:2948] Refusing ...ated
May 06 11:00:11 mesos mesos-master[1369]: I0506 11:00:11.088127  1377 master.cpp:2948] Refusing ...ated
May 06 11:00:30 mesos mesos-master[1369]: I0506 11:00:30.157085  1373 master.cpp:2948] Refusing ...ated
May 06 11:00:40 mesos mesos-master[1369]: I0506 11:00:40.970553  1374 master.cpp:2948] Refusing ...ated
May 06 11:00:43 mesos mesos-master[1369]: I0506 11:00:43.526232  1371 master.cpp:2948] Refusing ...ated
Hint: Some lines were ellipsized, use -l to show in full.
[centos@mesos ~]$ sudo service mesos-master status
Redirecting to /bin/systemctl status mesos-master.service
● mesos-master.service - Mesos Master
   Loaded: loaded (/usr/lib/systemd/system/mesos-master.service; enabled; vendor preset: disabled)
   Active: active (running) since Sun 2018-05-06 10:59:00 UTC; 1min 51s ago
 Main PID: 1342 (mesos-master)
   CGroup: /system.slice/mesos-master.service
           ├─1342 /usr/sbin/mesos-master --zk=zk://10.0.1.42:2181,10.0.1.203:2181,10.0.2.68:2181/mes...
           ├─1368 logger -p user.info -t mesos-master[1342]
           └─1369 logger -p user.err -t mesos-master[1342]

May 06 10:59:39 mesos mesos-master[1369]: W0506 10:59:39.484866  1371 master.cpp:9791] Possibly ...ve2)
May 06 10:59:39 mesos mesos-master[1369]: I0506 10:59:39.484937  1371 master.cpp:6890] Re-regist...000]
May 06 10:59:39 mesos mesos-master[1369]: I0506 10:59:39.485251  1371 hierarchical.cpp:574] Adde... ()}
May 06 10:59:39 mesos mesos-master[1369]: I0506 10:59:39.489727  1375 master.cpp:7265] Received ...s ()
May 06 10:59:39 mesos mesos-master[1369]: I0506 10:59:39.489774  1375 master.cpp:7359] Ignoring ...nges
May 06 10:59:44 mesos mesos-master[1369]: I0506 10:59:44.832376  1375 master.cpp:2948] Refusing ...ated
May 06 11:00:11 mesos mesos-master[1369]: I0506 11:00:11.088127  1377 master.cpp:2948] Refusing ...ated
May 06 11:00:30 mesos mesos-master[1369]: I0506 11:00:30.157085  1373 master.cpp:2948] Refusing ...ated
May 06 11:00:40 mesos mesos-master[1369]: I0506 11:00:40.970553  1374 master.cpp:2948] Refusing ...ated
May 06 11:00:43 mesos mesos-master[1369]: I0506 11:00:43.526232  1371 master.cpp:2948] Refusing ...ated
Hint: Some lines were ellipsized, use -l to show in full.
[centos@mesos ~]$
```

15. Similarly, check all the masters. Even if we have two masters running, it will be enough for us to perform ahead. Go on the **slave** tab, restart, and check the status of the service:

```
$ sudo service mesos-slave restart
$ sudo service mesos-slave status
```

16. Repeat this for all the agents.

So, we have now seen that the authentication-refused error was resolved by simply restarting all the masters. This means that if you have not provided any authentication, `mesos-master` will refuse all the unknown agents. Now let's set the principal without this, as we won't be able to start the Marathon service.

17. Go on the **Marathon** tab and type the following:

```
$ history |grep marathon.service
$ sudo vi /etc/systemd/system/multi-
user.target.wants/marathon.service
```

Beside e=marathon --
mesos_authentication_secret_file=/etc/default/mesos_authenticat
ion_secret, insert the following:

```
--mesos_authentication_principal=marathon1
```

18. Save and exit the file. Restart the server.

We have now seen how to enable authentication using secrets for the agents and the masters. In the next few sections, we will be learning how to enable **secured socket layer** (**SSL**) and secure our Mesos framework.

Enabling secured socket layer security

So far, we have seen how to secure the masters, agents, and our Mesos framework; we will now learn about securing Marathon. This will give you insight into enabling SSL, a protocol that is widely used in the security domain on our Mesos Marathon, and securing it by providing basic authentication mechanisms.

We will see how to make communication secure and limit the possibility of unauthorized interception of communication by enabling SSL.

Marathon enables you to secure its API endpoints via SSL and limit access to them with HTTP basic access authentication. It is advisable to use SSL if we are just enabling basic authentication to eliminate the possibility of data being accessed by third parties.

These are some simple steps to follow to enable SSL:

1. Generate the keystore using keytool
2. Use a self-signed certificate or if you can use an organization-wide trusted SSL certificate
3. Save the Marathon keystore configuration, this will include your password, the keystore path, and your credentials, such as username and password
4. Restart Marathon services

Check the service's response on the HTTPS port.

Generating marathon.jks file

Let's look at these steps in detail:

1. Go to **marathon1** tab in PuTTy and create a folder:

   ```
   $ cd /etc/marathon/ssl
   ```

2. Use `keytool` to generate the `marathon.jks` file:

   ```
   $ sudo keytool - keystore marathon.jks - deststorepass 123456 -
   alias marathon -genkey -keyalg RSA
   ```

3. Surprise! A few questions will pop up on your screen. Answer the questions and enter the password that we created in the preceding step. Here is a sample:

```
[centos@marathon1 ssl]$ sudo keytool -keystore marathon.jks -deststorepass 123456 -alias marathon -genk
ey -keyalg RSA
What is your first and last name?
  [Unknown]:  marathon
What is the name of your organizational unit?
  [Unknown]:  tutorial
What is the name of your organization?
  [Unknown]:  tetra
What is the name of your City or Locality?
  [Unknown]:  NY
What is the name of your State or Province?
  [Unknown]:  NY
What is the two-letter country code for this unit?
  [Unknown]:  US
Is CN=marathon, OU=tutorial, O=tetra, L=NY, ST=NY, C=US correct?
  [no]:  yes

Enter key password for <marathon>
        (RETURN if same as keystore password):

Warning:
The JKS keystore uses a proprietary format. It is recommended to migrate to PKCS12 which is an industry
 standard format using "keytool -importkeystore -srckeystore marathon.jks -destkeystore marathon.jks -d
eststoretype pkcs12".
[centos@marathon1 ssl]$ ls -rlt
total 4
-rw-r--r--. 1 root root 2214 May  7 10:22 marathon.jks
[centos@marathon1 ssl]$ 
```

We have successfully created the `marathon.jks` keystore.

Adding marathon.jks file in configuration

After creating a `marathon.jks` file, we will now add this to configuration:

1. Go to the default directory:

   $ cd /etc/default/

2. Edit the marathon file:

   $ sudo vi marathon

   You will see the following:

```
PuTTY Connection Manager   Connected to [centos@marathon1:/etc/default]
 marathon1
# For a description of the format, see: `man systemd.exec`, section
# `EnvironmentFile`.

# Available replacements
# see http://www.scala-sbt.org/sbt-native-packager/archetypes/systemloaders.html#override-start-script
# ---------------------------------------------------------------------
# Name                   Contains                    Current value
# (remove space)
# $ {{author}}           debian author               Mesosphere Package Builder <support@mesosphere.io
>
# $ {{descr}}            debian package description  Scheduler for Apache Mesos
# $ {{exec}}             startup script name         marathon
# $ {{chdir}}            app directory               /usr/share/marathon
# $ {{retries}}          retries for startup         0
# $ {{retryTimeout}}     retry timeout               60
# $ {{app_name}}         normalized app name         marathon
# $ {{app_main_class}}   main class/entry point      ${{app_main_class}}
# $ {{daemon_user}}      daemon user                 marathon
# $ {{daemon_group}}     daemon group                marathon
# ---------------------------------------------------------------------

# Setting JAVA_OPTS
# -----------------
# JAVA_OPTS="-Dpidfile.path=/var/run/marathon/play.pid"

# Setting PIDFILE
# ---------------
# PIDFILE="/var/run/marathon/play.pid"

-- INSERT --
```

3. At the end of the line, where you see the cursor in the screenshot, insert the following parameters:

```
MARATHON_SSL_KEYSTORE_PATH=/etc/marathon/ssl/marathon.jks
MARATHON_SSL_KEYSTORE_PASSWORD=123456
MARATHON_HTTP_CREDENTIALS=admin:password
```

If you look carefully, in the marathon `keystore` path, you can see we have appended a path where we have stored the `marathon.jks` keystore, the password, and the credential you want. Here, `admin` is the username and `password` is the password

4. Save and exit using `:wq!`
5. Restart the marathon services:

```
$ sudo service marathon restart
```

6. Check the status of the services:

```
$ sudo service marathon status
$ sudo service marathon status -l
```

You will need to wait until all the services get started. Check for this on your screen:

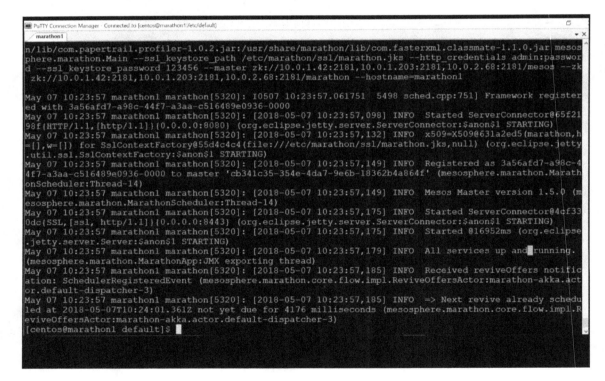

7. Go to the browser and check whether we have configured properly. Key in the `https://marathon1:8443` address.

   You will see that our connection is not private as we are using self-signed certificates:

8. Click on **ADVANCED,** as shown in the preceding screenshot, and then click **proceed to marathon1**. You will get the following screen:

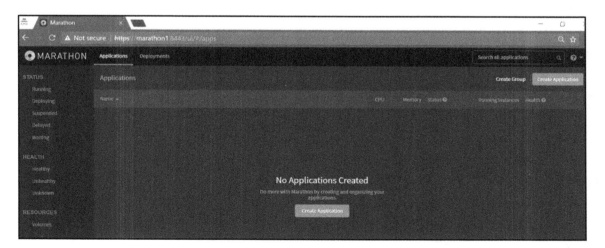

We have now logged into the Marathon console.

9. But are you wondering why it didn't ask for a password? This is because this console was cached in your browser; to test that, you can copy and paste the path of the console in an incognito tab, a private tab, or on another browser where this console is not cached, then clear your cache and restart the browser, and you will see the following:

10. Enter **Username** as `admin` and **Password** as `password`.

Now we have seen how simple it was to configure SSL security in Marathon using basic authentication and self-signed certificates, and hence our communication is sure to be encrypted and we can avoid attacks, such as man-in-the-middle, wherein people with malicious intent can intercept our messages.

Summary

Hopefully, this chapter has given you some basic information about securing Mesos. We learned how to enable authenticators, and configure our masters and agents with secrets and credentials so that they can build trust relationships. We saw how we can easily add a self-signed SSL certificate to Marathon and secure all our communications. In the next chapter, we will be learning about Marathon-lb and how to deploy the Apache web server and Cassandra server.

Managing Resources in Mesos

8

Software deployment plays a very important role in the success the development of any application. Your application might run fine on your computer, but that doesn't mean that it is really ready for others to use. In order to make your application more user-friendly and to protect it from piracy, you will need to add the required features to your program. Here, we'll make use of one deployment technique, known as the blue/green deployment technique, with Marathon-LB. Blue/green deployment is a technique that uses two identical production environments, called blue and green, to reduce downtime and the risks of running applications at the production stage. At any time, only one of the environments is live, serving all production traffic.

In this chapter, we will cover the following topics:

- Understanding Marathon-LB
- Deploying an Apache web server
- Deploying a Cassandra server
- Understanding the failover mechanism

Marathon-LB

Marathon-LB is a tool for managing HAProxy that works by consuming Marathon's app state. HAProxy is a fast, efficient, battle-tested, highly available load balancer with many advanced features that power a number of high-profile websites. Marathon-LB provides a Python script that performs zero-downtime applications deployments. It helps you to safely deploy applications serving live traffic by creating two versions of an application: blue and green.

Let's see how it is done:

1. To perform an application update, the green version is deployed, while all customer requests are sent to the blue version.
2. Once the green version is deployed and healthy, the load balancer can start draining connections from the blue version and instead sends customer requests to the green version.
3. The blue version of the application can be deleted once all customer requests are being directed to the green version.

So, let's understand the overall procedure as follows:

1. The Marathon-LB script `marathon_lb.py` connects to the Marathon API to retrieve all running apps, then generates a HAProxy config file, and finally, reloads HAProxy.
2. Here, if you add one or more hosts in your application, you don't have to restart your load balancer. HAProxy will automatically generate the config and reload HAProxy, which will make your new host available to serve the traffic.
3. By default, Marathon-LB binds to the service port of every application and sends incoming requests to the application instances.
4. Services are exposed on the service port, as defined in their Marathon definition. Apps are only exposed on LBs that have the same LB tag (or group) as defined in the Marathon app's labels (using `HAPROXY_GROUP`).

Installing Marathon-LB

In this example, we will perform a blue/green deployment technique using the `zdd.py` Python script and special Marathon-LB labels in your application definitions.

You need to first install Marathon-LB, using a Docker image, by executing the following command:

```
docker run -d -p 9090:9090
```

As you can see in the preceding command, `9090` is the port to which your HAProxy will bind—you access the HAProxy web page to find out the status of your load balancer. Then, next is `-p 8081:10001`. This is where your services will run. Here, we set it to `10000` and `8081`. So, we have exposed the `8081` port where your application will get accessed; and inside Docker, `10000` will be used. So, this is how your port mapping will happen. After that, we defined `--add-host`.

This variable needs to be defined if you don't have any DNS. If you have DNS in your environment, you can skip this; your environment will make use of a DNS to resolve the hostname. Here, the hostname and IP address are defined manually, in a way that is understood by Docker. After that, -e is PORTS, which we have already mapped with 9090, which will bind the HAProxy. Then we have the Docker image marathon-lb. We also have SSE mode defined, in which Marathon-LB will connect to the Marathon endpoints to inspect the change in state of the application, after which we defined the Marathon URL. Marathon-LB will now connect to this port and IP address to inspect the state of the application.

By executing the --group external command, we define a group here. So, when we deploy the application inside our Mesos cluster, we'll need to define one global parameter with the external command. As we saw earlier, we need to define one command tag that Marathon-LB will use for deploying the application via Marathon, and examine the application state to start reporting on the application inside the Marathon-LB web console. So, let's hit *Enter*, and you will get a long UID.

You can run the following command line to check the application state:

```
sudo docker ps -a
```

Here, you can see the results of the preceding command that we just ran:

```
[centos@marathon1 ~]$ sudo docker ps -a
CONTAINER ID        IMAGE                    COMMAND                CREATED          STATUS                     PO
RTS                                                                                  NAMES
8d41f336afb0        mesosphere/marathon-lb   "tini -g -- /marathoâ¦"  12 seconds ago   Up 11 seconds              8
0/tcp, 443/tcp, 9091/tcp, 0.0.0.0:9090->9090/tcp, 0.0.0.0:8081->10000/tcp   clever_dubinsky
18b782a385cb        mesosphere/marathon-lb   "tini -g -- /marathoâ¦"  22 hours ago     Exited (143) 21 hours ago
                                                                                     flamboyant_borg
9d7e1ff012e1        mesosphere/marathon-lb   "tini -g -- /marathoâ¦"  22 hours ago     Exited (143) 22 hours ago
                                                                                     boring_leakev
```

You can also remove another one, if it isn't required, by executing the following command line:

```
sudo docker rm 18b782a385cb
```

This will give you the following results:

```
[centos@marathon1 ~]$ sudo docker rm 18b782a385cb 9d7e1ff012e1
18b782a385cb
9d7e1ff012e1
```

You can now check if another one has been removed by again executing this command:

```
sudo docker ps -a
```

So, let's quickly browse to port 9090. You can even check the logs by executing the following command:

```
sudo docker logs 8d41f336afb0
```

This is what you can see in the logs. You won't see any errors here, so let's quickly browse to the HAProxy page, which is http://marathon1:9090/haproxy?stats. You won't get to see any applications listed here, as we have not deployed anything via Marathon in our Mesos cluster:

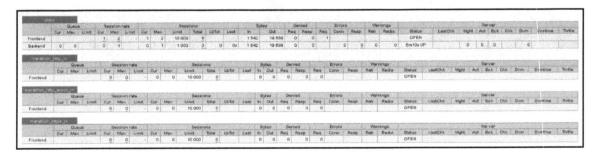

So, let's quickly understand what we are doing here:

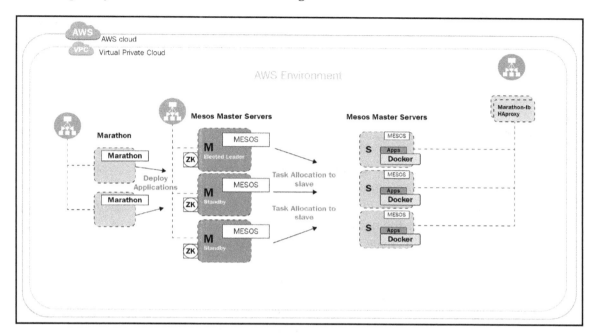

As you can see in the preceding diagram, we have three **Mesos Master Servers**, three **Mesos Slave Servers**, and two **Marathon** master servers. We are going to install a **Marathon-lb HAproxy** server, and will have Elastic Load Balancer to serve the traffic.

Implementing the blue/green deployment with Marathon-LB

Let's go ahead and start deploying the application to understand how blue/green deployment works, by performing the following steps:

1. We will create a new version of the web application that uses the nginx web server, as well as creating a definition file to deploy the nginx web server on our Mesos cluster using Marathon.

2. We should focus on the following two new labels used for managing the blue/green deployment technique:
    - HAPROXY_DEPLOYMENT_GROUP: This label uniquely identifies a pair of apps belonging to a blue/green deployment, and will be used as the app name in the HAProxy configuration.
    - HAPROXY_DEPLOYMENT_ALT_PORT: An alternate service port is required because Marathon requires service ports to be unique across all apps.
3. Then, we will install Python version 3, as required by zdd.py, Git, and our other dependencies.
4. Then, we will clone the Marathon-LB repository to get the zdd.py script.
5. Use the zdd.py script for deploying the application.
6. Validate the deployed services on Marathon and browse to the HAProxy page on the browser to see the nginx web server page.
7. After that, we will create a new version of our web application that uses the Apache web server instead of nginx.
8. Use the ZDD web-UI script to perform a zero-downtime deployment with a new version of the application.
9. So, without any downtime, we will replace the nginx web server with the Apache web server. We will see how this can be handled using Marathon-LB zero-downtime deployment.
10. Then we will return to the console and validate the progress, and reload the browser page. While browsing the page, we will discover how easily we deployed the Apache web server without any downtime.

So, let's quickly go for a demo by performing the following steps:

1. Create a definition file for our nginx web server by executing the following command line:

```
sudo vi nginx.json
```

The preceding command line will generate the following output:

```
marathon1    marathon2    master1    master2    master3    slave1
{
  "id": "web",
  "container": {
    "type": "DOCKER",
    "docker": {
      "image": "nginx",
      "network": "BRIDGE",
      "portMappings": [
        {
          "hostPort": 0,
          "containerPort": 80,
          "servicePort": 10000
        }
      ],
      "forcePullImage": true
    }
  },
  "instances": 4,
  "cpus": 0.1,
  "mem": 65,
  "healthChecks": [
    {
      "protocol": "MESOS_HTTP",
      "path": "/",
      "portIndex": 0,
      "timeoutSeconds": 15,
      "gracePeriodSeconds": 15,
      "intervalSeconds": 3,
      "maxConsecutiveFailures": 10
    }
  ],
  "labels": {
    "HAPROXY_DEPLOYMENT_GROUP": "web",
-- INSERT --
```

As you can see in the preceding screenshot, this is the definition file we have created. Here, you will see the container port is 80, and the service port is 10000, which was defined earlier while creating our Marathon-LB container. We have defined our instances as 4, our CPUs at 0.1, and memory at 65. Spot the healthChecks parameter we have added here, and, most importantly, the labels. We have already defined HAPROXY_DEPLOYMENT_GROUP as web. Then, our HAPROXY_DEPLOYMENT_ALT_PORT is 10001. So, for blue/green deployment, it will use the 10001 port. As you have seen, we have defined HAPROXY_GROUP, which is external, while creating our Marathon-LB container. Let's quickly save this. With this, we are done with our first step of creating the nginx definition.

2. Our next step is to install Python. Hit the command line to check your Python version, we already have 2.7.5 Python installed.

3. Exit using the exit command, or by pressing *Ctrl + D*.

4. Now, install the supported tools by executing the following command line:

```
sudo yum installgit gcc openssl-devel and libcurl-devel
```

So, these are the supported tools required. Now, clear the screen.

5. Enter the following command:

```
export PYCURL_SSL_LIBRARY=nss
```

6. Now add some add-on packages using the following command:

```
sudo yum install epel-release
```

7. Use the following command to install pip:

```
sudo yum install python-pip
```

8. Let's upgrade pip by executing the following command line:

```
sudo pip install -upgrade pip
```

9. Install some of the required dependencies by using the following command:

```
sudo pip install requests six jwt
```

The preceding command line will install the required dependencies, as shown in the following screenshot:

As you can see in the preceding screenshot, the required dependencies were installed with some errors, which can be ignored. Clear the screen.

10. Now, enter the following command:

```
sudo pip install pycurl –global-option="-with-nss"
```

These are the dependencies required to run our `zdd.py` script.

11. Let's clone the Marathon-LB repository using the `git clone`, by executing the following command:

```
git clone https://github.com/mesosphere/marathon-lb.git
```

We already have `marathon-lb` installed.

12. Run the `ls -rlt` command, which will fetch the Marathon app from the `marathon-lb` folder. You will see the `marathon-lb` folder as your present directory.

13. Let's install the `python-jwt` module, which is again required to run your Python script:

```
sudo yum install  python-jwt
```

We already have this module, but you have to make sure you install it.

14. After installing dependency tools, let's run your zero-deployment script. This is the script that we will run:

```
zdd.pynginx.json
```

We have already created this file. It has all the definitions required to run the nginx web server.

Here, we have your master IP, and this is our Marathon-LB IP with port 9090, which you have seen while running the LB container earlier. Let's hit *Enter* to quickly troubleshoot this. So here, we have got data that shows Connection refused. This is because we have defined the incorrect IP address, which is 10.0.1.42, hence, we need to define the correct Marathon IP as we have defined Marathon-LB here. In our case, our IP address will be the same, but if you are using a different server, your IP will get changed. So, let's quickly clear this screen, and start this process from top:

1. Correct the IP address in the following command line, and hit the *Enter* key:

```
./marathon-lbzdd.py -j nginx.json -m http://10.0.1.191:8080 -f -1
http://10.0.1.191:9090 --syslog-socker /dev/null
```

The preceding command line will generate the following output:

```
],
"id": "/web-blue",
"instances": 4,
"labels": {
  "HAPROXY_0_PORT": "10000",
  "HAPROXY_APP_ID": "web",
  "HAPROXY_DEPLOYMENT_ALT_PORT": "10001",
  "HAPROXY_DEPLOYMENT_COLOUR": "blue",
  "HAPROXY_DEPLOYMENT_GROUP": "web",
  "HAPROXY_DEPLOYMENT_NEW_INSTANCES": "0",
  "HAPROXY_DEPLOYMENT_STARTED_AT": "2018-05-21T19:52:56.904999",
  "HAPROXY_DEPLOYMENT_TARGET_INSTANCES": "4",
  "HAPROXY_GROUP": "external"
},
"mem": 65
```

In the preceding screenshot, the important part is the labels that we have here. The HAProxy port reads the web, and the deployment color is blue, so currently, we are in blue deployment.

2. Let's quickly go to your Marathon console, where you can see your **web-blue** application got deployed on the `mesos-slave1` server:

3. This is the `mesos-slave1` server. Now, you can refresh this, and you will see your web is running on port `10000`:

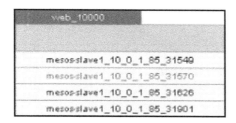

4. When you browse your application, you will see we have deployed the blue ID, which is **web-blue**:

5. Access this application via our Elastic Load Balancer on AWS, and validate the Elastic Load Balancer, which you can see is already set up and named `wordpress-lb`.

6. Now click on the **Target Groups** tab on the left, and you can see we have created the target groups here with the name `wordpress-lb`, which is our `marathon1` server on port `8081`:

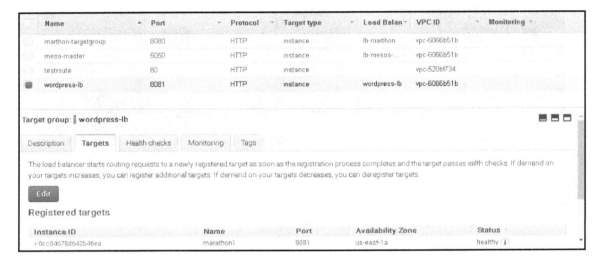

7. Now, click on **Load Balancers** to see the description on the left.
8. Copy the **DNS** name from the **Description** tab and paste it into your browser. You will see the **Welcome to nginx!** landing page, which means we have successfully installed the nginx app on our Mesos cluster:

Deploying an Apache web server

Now that we have explored the blue deployment technique, let's learn something about the green deployment via an example.

Let's go to our Marathon console, and then type the following command to get the total number of files present:

```
ls -rlt
```

Let's open the `nginx.json` file using the following commands:

```
$ sudo cp nginx.json apache.json
$ ls -rlt
```

Now, let's open the `apache.json` file using the following command line:

```
vi apache.json
```

In this file, we need to change the `image` to `httpd` to create `apache.json` with HTTP, and save it with `:wq!`. Then we execute the `cat Apache.json` command to read the file.

Next we will go ahead and deploy the JSON file to see the results. As you can see in the following screenshot, once you deploy this JSON file, it will slowly and gradually deploy the `httpd`, and will remove the existing nginx deployment:

Hit the *Enter* key.

You will see it's a `green` deployment.

Now, let's go to our console. Go to the application, and you will see the green deployment in progress:

You will also still see your application gets sent to the nginx server. Try to open your nginx page and open it on the marathon1 server, and you will see that your app is still responding:

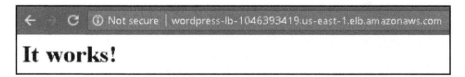

You can see that currently, it's running using one CPU, and will slowly and gradually deploy `web-green` to `0.4` and `web-blue` to `0.1`.

Here, the existing app is running four instances, while the new app is running only one instance. You will see the update's status progress, as well, stating that `There are 1 draining listeners, about to kill the following tasks.`

After scaling down the old app by one instance, and scaling up the new app by two instances, you will see the output, showing the old app running three instances, and the new app running two instances, in our console.

You will see the `web-green` app is running two instances. And it's running three instances on the console, which is going to reduce the blue app (existing) and increase the green app (new). This is how blue/green deployment works. Without any downtime, it will automatically rotate the app. As you will see, our green app has been moved to 4. And old is reduced to 2, which will slowly vanish later.

Eventually, you will see a message displaying `About to delete old app /web-blue.` Now, on the console, you will see that only the `web-green` app is running. So, let's quickly browse the `web-green` page on our incognito browser, which is our load balancer URL, and we get `It works!`:

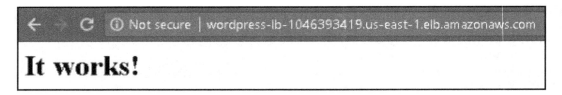

As shown in the preceding screenshot, this is httpd landing page.

So, we have installed Apache httpd as a green deployment. So now, what if you want to redeploy to an alternative deployment, as we did from blue to green earlier? To do so, check that the current status of your application is the green deployment. If you run that script again with the nginx web server definition, it will show you the blue deployments.

Let's quickly see now how this is done. Type this command and hit the *Enter* key:

```
$ ./marathon-lb/zdd.py -j nginx.json -m http://10.0.1.191:8080 -f -1
http://10.0.1.191:9090 -socket /dev/null
```

You will get the output shown in the following screenshot:

```
],
"id": "/web-blue",
"instances": 1,
"labels": {
  "HAPROXY_0_PORT": "10000",
  "HAPROXY_APP_ID": "web",
  "HAPROXY_DEPLOYMENT_ALT_PORT": "10001",
  "HAPROXY_DEPLOYMENT_COLOUR": "blue",
  "HAPROXY_DEPLOYMENT_GROUP": "web",
  "HAPROXY_DEPLOYMENT_NEW_INSTANCES": "0",
  "HAPROXY_DEPLOYMENT_STARTED_AT": "2018-05-21T20:42:00.463650",
  "HAPROXY_DEPLOYMENT_TARGET_INSTANCES": "4",
  "HAPROXY_GROUP": "external"
},
```

You will see that the green deployment is already detected, so it says `blue`.

So now, it will start the blue instances and drain the green instances, and you will see that the `web-blue` deployment is initiated. The one instance is upon `slave2`, which will drain the existing app that is green and scale the blue app, as shown here:

So in this way, the user can see the application, which still works without any downtime because your current application is not yet migrated.

Now if you see your application, it still works. This is still in the scaling phase where it will drain the existing one, and then will make the new deployment go live.

Zero-downtime deployment (ZDD)

Now that you've seen how the blue/green deployment works, let's understand the traffic splitting between the blue and green versions of the app. So, ZDD has support to split the traffic between two versions of the same app (that is, the blue version and the green version) by having instances of both versions live at the same time. This is supported by the `HAPROXY_DEPLOYMENT_NEW_INSTANCES` label. When you run ZDD with the `--new-instances` flag, it creates only the specified number of instances of the new app, and deletes the same number of instances from the old app. For example, if your blue deployment is running with the full wrap and the `--new-instances` flag, it shows 2. So, it will just delete the existing two apps and will run the new app with new instances.

So, for example, consider the same nginx app example, where there are 10 instances of nginx running image version 1. Now we can use ZDD to create two instances of version 2, and retain 8 instances of version 1, so that traffic is split in a 80:20 ratio. Creating two instances of the new version automatically deletes two instances of the existing version by adding the `--new-instances 2` flag. This state, where you have instances of both old and new versions of the same app live at the same time, is called a hybrid state. When a deployment group is in a hybrid state, it needs to be converted completely into either the current version or the previous version, before deploying any further versions. This could be done with the help of the `--complete-cur` and `--complete-prev` flags in ZDD. So, let's quickly perform this demo to understand how the traffic splitting happens between the blue and green apps, and how you can convert the hybrid state completely to the current or previous version of the app. So now, you can see our `web-blue` app is completely installed. Let's split the traffic between the blue and green apps. We will install the Apache server and change the IP address to `10.0.1.191`. We need to run this `--new-instances 2`:

```
$ ./marathon-lb/zdd.py -j apache.json -m http://10.0.1.191:8080 -f -l
http://10.0.1.191:9090 -syslog-socket /dev/null --new-instances 2
```

So here, our traffic will be split between four instances, of which two instances will be `blue`, and two instances will be `green`. Hit the *Enter* key:

```
"id": "/web-green",
"instances": 1,
"labels": {
  "HAPROXY_0_PORT": "10000",
  "HAPROXY_APP_ID": "web",
  "HAPROXY_DEPLOYMENT_ALT_PORT": "10001",
  "HAPROXY_DEPLOYMENT_COLOUR": "green",
  "HAPROXY_DEPLOYMENT_GROUP": "web",
  "HAPROXY_DEPLOYMENT_NEW_INSTANCES": "2",
  "HAPROXY_DEPLOYMENT_STARTED_AT": "2018-05-21T20:56:41.777843",
  "HAPROXY_DEPLOYMENT_TARGET_INSTANCES": "4",
  "HAPROXY_GROUP": "external"
},
"mem": 65
```

Here, you will see the HAPROXY_DEPLOYMENT_NEW_INSTANCES flag is enabled with 2; and your deployment color is green.

Here our green app has been deployed-currently, there is only one instance. So let's wait until it scales to put the app up to two instances, and then try accessing the website.

You will see the nginx page, because we have again deployed green to blue. So once the current installation is completed, we will see our request flows between Apache and nginx.

Here, you will see your traffic is split between the green and blue apps, so keep on refreshing and watch how it works.

So for now, you can either roll back to your existing app, or you can complete your current app deployment, using the flags that we saw earlier. Those flags are --complete-cur and --complete-prev. If you want to complete with the current deployment, you need to run the command again with the --complete-cur flag to delete the existing old app. This will create two more instances. If you want to deploy the application or roll back to the previous application, or if you don't want to go with the current deployment, you just have to use the --complete-prev command.

You have two instances of the blue app and two instances of the green app. You have to decide whether you need to roll back or continue with your current deployment. You can validate your URL, which is your load balancer URL, to see if your traffic is splitting or not.

Sometimes it goes to nginx, and you will be able see your HAProxy reloading, as per the status change from your application:

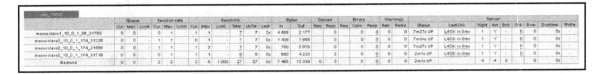

So here, we're executing the `--complete-cur` command. Our current deployment was our Apache deployment, which was green.

Let's hit the *Enter* key. It will display `Considering blue color as existing app and green color as new app`, giving you some information: `Existing app running 2 instances, new app running 2 instances`.

This will convert your app from split to only a single one, which is your green environment. Then it displays `Scaling new app up to 4 instances`.

Let's go to our Marathon console, and you will see that our `web-green` app has been scaled to four, as per our definition of `--complete-cur`. This is going to be trained now.

Let's check your statistics on HAProxy, as follows:

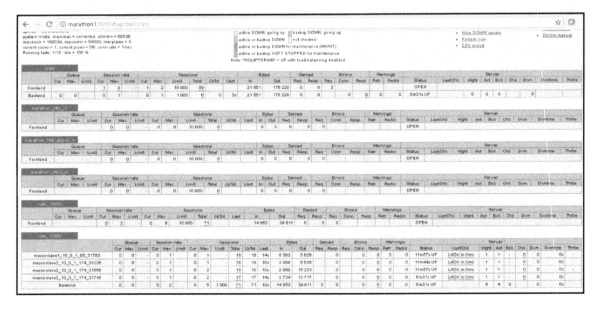

As you can see, these two are going to drain now, displaying `About to delete old app /web-blue`.

So let's quickly go to our console, and validate. You can see our green app is now with four instances and our blue app is deleted now.

So, that's how you can use multiple development environments as per your requirements. Next, we will learn how to deploy Cassandra on Apache Mesos. Before we start, we first need to understand what Cassandra is.

What is Cassandra?

Apache Cassandra is an open source, distributed database management system. It is designed to handle large amounts of data across many commodity servers. It provides high availability, with no single point of failure. Cassandra offers robust support for clusters spanning multiple data centers, with asynchronous masterless replication allowing low latency operation for all clients. It is extremely fault-tolerant because of its built-in replication features. It is also highly performant, decentralized, and most importantly, it's extremely durable for companies that cannot afford to lose any data.

Any distributed persistent application including Cassandra can have challenges. Let's understand few of those challenges that we face: complexity of installation; data movement expense and manual processes with node failures; performance limited by direct attached storage.

Before we begin our demo, let's first understand how Cassandra overcomes these challenges through running inside the Docker. That is we will be running Cassandra inside Docker, and then the Docker containers will be deployed on top of Mesos cluster, which means we are going to deploy Apache Cassandra image via Marathon; and using Marathon, it will get deployed on your Mesos cluster. It will leverage an external storage platform for its persistent data. We will be using REX-Ray and EBS volume. REX-Ray is a volume driver that will connect with your external storage. We are going to use AWS EBS for our persistent data. If by any chance our server goes down or if our Docker container crashes, it will automatically get started on any other server, and the same persistent data will get attached automatically, using your REX-Ray volume driver.

So, let's quickly go ahead and perform some activity on how to deploy Apache Cassandra on your Mesos cluster via Marathon.

Deploying of a Cassandra cluster

Let's see how we can deploy an Apache Cassandra cluster on our Apache Mesos cluster using the Marathon framework. Before we start, let's quickly review our two JSON files, which will create one Cassandra container each on our Apache Mesos cluster. Let's check our JSON files:

```json
{
  "id": "/cassandra1",
  "cmd": null,
  "cpus": 1,
  "mem": 8000,
  "disk": 0,
  "instances": 1,
  "constraints": [
    [
      "hostname",
      "UNIQUE"
    ]
  ],
  "acceptedResourceRoles": [
    "*"
  ],
  "container": {
    "type": "DOCKER",
    "docker": {
      "forcePullImage": true,
      "image": "cassandra",
      "parameters": [
        {
          "key": "env",
          "value": "CASSANDRA_CLUSTERNAME=cassandra-cluster"
        },
        {
          "key": "env",
          "value": "CASSANDRA_SEEDS=10.0.1.85,10.0.1.174,10.0.1.203"
        },
        {
          "key": "volume-driver",
          "value": "rexray/ebs"
```

You can see that we have the id as cassandra1, which is our container. We are not using cmd command hence, "cmd": null. We have defined cpus as 1, and memory is around 8 GB. We have not defined any disk, as we will be using external storage, which is AWS EBS. We wull also define instances as 1, and constraints is UNIQUE, as we will use a unique server to deploy these Cassandra images. We will use DOCKER as our container type, and the image will be cassandra. This will pull the cassandra image from Docker Hub. Then, we have defined some environments: CASSANDRA_CLUSTERNAME, CASSANDRA_SEEDS, and the most important part, the volume-driver. We are using the rexray/ebs volume driver, which is for AWS EBS. This will create a volume on our AWS. The volume will be defined as data1, and will be mounted to var/lib/cassandra. We will keep the rest as default. Next, we'll deploy the JSON file using curl and hit *Enter*:

```
curl -X POST http://marathon1:8080/v2/apps -d @cassendra1.json -H "Content-
type: application/json"
```

Let's check our Marathon web console here, you will see cassandra1 was deployed.

This JSON file will run on mesos-master2, which is our slave server; refresh the page and you will see the volumes and the data when a volume has been created. Now we will run another JSON file, which means we will be deploying two Cassandra servers in the cluster.

To deploy the second Cassandra server, we will be following the same procedure as we did for the cassandra1.json file. Before we deploy the file, let's check the JSON file to verify whether instances is 1.

After deploying the JSON file, go to the console and you will see cassandra2 deployed. You can check your EBS volume, the data-persistent volume it has created, and you will find that the data2 volume of 16 GB has been created. Here, we have two servers in the cluster. Let's log in to the Cassandra server and validate these clusters. First, log in to master2 and enter the sudo docker ps -a command. This should show you the whole Cassandra cluster.

Enter the same command under slave1, and you will find the Cassandra server has been deployed.

Now, enter this command:

```
sudo docker exec -it  c70a97cfd470 cqlsh
```

Here, cqlsh is a Cassandra client to connect to your Cassandra server. You will be able to connect.

Next, repeat the preceding mentioned command for `slave1` and enter the `describe keyspaces` command. When you initialize the database, it will show that there are five keyspaces created. Now, we will be creating a new keyspace in `master2`, and check if it gets replicated on `slave1` or not. To check that, we need to enter the following command:

```
create keyspace devtest WITH replication = {'class': 'Strategy name',
'replication_factor' :1};
```

Here, we created a `devtest` keyspace. Check the keyspace created using the `describe` command. We need to check this also on `slave1`. As you can see, it got replicated automatically across another server.

We will also create one more keyspace using the `create keyspace` command. This will be `devtest1`, which is created on `slave1` too.

Now, let's check if any changes made in `slave1` are reflected in the `master` too. In `slave1`, we will create a keyspace, say, `production`, using the following command:

```
create keyspace devtest WITH replication = {'class': 'Strategy name',
'replication_factor' :1};
```

This will create the keyspace. Now, to check the newly created keyspace, run `describe keyspaces` on `slave1`, as well as on `master2`. You will find the keyspace got replicated in `master2`.

This is how the Apache Cassandra works in clusters. Now, let's understand how the failover mechanism works here.

Failover mechanism

To check the failover mechanism, we will first go to `master2`, and stop the Docker instances using the following command:

```
sudo docker stop (Container ID)
```

Here, you can check in Marathon that `cassandra1` has stopped.

On refreshing the page, you can see it has created the instance on master2, where we have stopped it. This is done automatically. Here, the scenario where we have seen one of the containers went down and a backup was automatically created. Now, let's validate this by running the following command:

```
sudo docker ps -a
```

You will find that your old container is down, and the new one, which was created automatically, will be up.

What happens if your server is down? For example, let's shut down our master2 server. To do that, let's go to AWS console, then EC2 **Instances**, click on master2 server, stop the server. On the Marathon app, you can see the failure gets detected. As you are aware, we have stopped the master2 server, but our slave and Cassandra are both up and running. We can verify this by checking the keyspaces. You will notice there is no impact here. This is how the failover will be managed. We can call this high availability, such that if one server went down, the other server can still serve requests.

You must have noticed that, as soon as I stopped the mesos-master2, our Marathon also went down.

This happened as our master1 server was already in a shutdown state, and we also closed our master2 server, which was why the marathon was not able to detect the available master. Let's now start all the master servers. Here, we considered master2 as our slave, and master1 as our server. Keep in mind here that we need to keep the server and slave separate.

Consider one more scenario. For example, if we stop or shut down the slave servers, any instance of a container running on the slave instance will get started on another server automatically. Let's replicate this scenario. Let's go to the Marathon app, and you can see our cassandra1 and cassandra2 instances are automatically up as soon as we started our mesos server which is on slave2 and slave1. As you are aware, our Docker container was running on master2, which is slave1, and as soon as slave1 shuts down, the application started running under the slave2 server. Let's check what happens when we shut down slave2. Verify that the cluster is up and running by visiting the Mesos page. You will notice that there is no cluster name present in master3. To add a cluster name, we need to update the IP as our EC2 public IP.

After the IP is updated, you can check that all three master servers are up. This shows how the Cassandra server worked and served the customer, even though our master servers were down, and the server again went to the node once the masters were up again. Now, let's check with a scenario where we shut down the slave server, and see how the Cassandra server behaves.

You can see in the Mesos framework that the one Mesos server has two slave servers: `slave2`, and `slave1`, the latter of which is where the Cassandra server is running. First, stop `slave1` instances. Here, we will see how our Cassandra container will get stopped; and it will get enabled under the server with the same persistent data storage enabled. It will automatically attach the EBS volume to the new server. Once `slave2` has stopped, check on the Marathon app and you will find that the problem with the server was detected. Within no time, the `master2` server got activated automatically and is in the running state. Now let's start `slave1` again, and shut down `slave2`. Once `slave1` is up and running, go to **slave1-log in** and check the process. But before this, you will have to enable `docker start` first. This can also be done by adding your startup script, so that when your server is restarted, and Docker will start automatically start. The recommended practice is that it should start automatically during a server restart. On running the following command, you should be shown the exited process:

```
Sudo docker ps -a
```

If you want you can remove this process, do so using the `sudo docker rm` command. Now let's stop the `slave2` server. Wait until it gets stopped. Wait for a few seconds for Marathon to detect this. You will notice that it has detected the failure and our Cassandra has started working on slave1. This is how we can check and test the failover. So let's go to the server and validate this. On our `slave1` server, enter `sudo docker ps -a`, and you will be able to find our Cassandra image. You can check our container by using the following command:

```
sudo docker exec -it {container ID} cqlsh
```

You will enter `cqlsh`, and now you can verify the keyspaces by using the following command:

```
describe keyspaces
```

You will notice the `production` keyspace, `devtest`, and `devtest1` are available. This show that even if your server is down, the Cassandra database continues to work automatically. It has also attached the external storage, which is AWS EBS, with the help of the REX-Ray volume driver.

This is how you can deploy the Cassandra database on a Mesos cluster. You can not only attach a Cassandra database, but any other database as well, including MySQL or Spark, or any other tool for which you want high availability, which is often mission-critical for businesses. You can deploy it on Apache Mesos and take advantage of this.

Summary

In this chapter, we explored blue/green deployment, and also saw how we can use this technique to deploy our application safely using Marathon-LB. We also learned how to deploy an Apache web server and a Cassandra server on Apache Mesos. We also tested a few failover mechanisms that can be used to provide high availability for our server, which will be beneficial for the business.

Another Book You May Enjoy

If you enjoyed this book, you may be interested in another book by Packt:

Apache Mesos Cookbook
David Blomquist

ISBN: 9781785884627

- Set up Mesos on different operating systems
- Use the Marathon and Chronos frameworks to manage multiple applications
- Work with Mesos and Docker
- Integrate Mesos with Spark and other big data frameworks
- Use networking features in Mesos for effective communication between containers
- Configure Mesos for high availability using Zookeeper
- Secure your Mesos clusters with SASL and Authorization ACLs
- Solve everyday problems and discover the best practices

Leave a review - let other readers know what you think

Please share your thoughts on this book with others by leaving a review on the site that you bought it from. If you purchased the book from Amazon, please leave us an honest review on this book's Amazon page. This is vital so that other potential readers can see and use your unbiased opinion to make purchasing decisions, we can understand what our customers think about our products, and our authors can see your feedback on the title that they have worked with Packt to create. It will only take a few minutes of your time, but is valuable to other potential customers, our authors, and Packt. Thank you!

Index

www.ingramcontent.com/pod-product-compliance
Lightning Source LLC
Chambersburg PA
CBHW080637060326
40690CB00021B/4973